PRAISE FOR *ALWAYS*

D1089674

Mesmerizing. The prose is lean and elliptical, full of sur-
prising, insightful turns. Paul and Hal's suggestively drawn
intermittent friendship darkly enchants. Newark and its
inhabitants are vivid in their various degrees of ruin. Father
and son scenes unfold in unexpected, superbly convincing
ways. Sexy, perilous, lost Hal in particular is a marvelous
creation. I hated to see this story end.

—Paul Russell, author of
The Unreal Life of Sergey Nobokov
and *War Against the Animals*

A gritty coming-of-age novel that rings true on every page.
Through the story of two working-class kids in 1960s New
Jersey, Dellaguzzo offers a vivid portrait of a time and a
way of life that are distinct in themselves and yet univer-
sally resonant. . . . With a strong ear for dialogue and
characters who jump off the page, this book feels genuinely
lived, unadorned by the rose-colored lens of nostalgia.

—Lewis DeSimone, author of *Channeling Morgan*

A harrowing story of two boys grasping for connection in
an era when gay desire and brutality were inextricably
bound. Dellaguzzo's prose has a gritty lyricism all its own,
finding poetry in New Jersey streets and bars and alleys,
which gives the book the ring of authenticity but also con-
jures the fevered passion of myth.

—James Sie, author of *Still Life Las Vegas*

Reminiscent of John Knowles' *A Separate Peace*, Lou Dellaguzzo's *Always There by Leaving* follows Paul and Hal through a decaying 1960s Newark, where the ostracized adolescents' alliance begins with a fist fight and grows with fits and starts of sexual tension, dangerous dares, and deadly consequences. Dellaguzzo captures the dynamics of working-class characters, teenage angst, dissociation, and relationship turmoil with a sharp, passionate style, rendering a story of two unlikely friends who find in each other an unlikely hero, and a novel today's readers will find a new classic.

—Chip Livingston, author of *Crow Blue, Crow Black* and *Naming Ceremony*

CRITICAL ACCLAIM FOR LOU DELLAGUZZO

[T]here is a pressured elegance to all the writing. These yesterdays of gay life remain vivid and salty sharp here, and description often doubles as insight.
—*Lambda Literary Foundation*

One of the most exciting queer writers around today. His work is astounding.
—Shaun Levin, author of *Snapshots*

Lou Dellaguzzo crafts stories like an ice sculptor, turning opaque blocks of everyday life into crystalline vignettes, until, whether in trouble or in triumph, out pours the secret light of a gay man.
—Martin Pousson, author of *Black Sheep Boy*

Always There

by Leaving

Always There
by Leaving

Lou Dellaguzzo

Beautiful Dreamer Press

Beautiful Dreamer Press
309 Cross Street
Nevada City, CA 95959
U.S.A.
www.BeautifulDreamerPress.com
info@BeautifulDreamerPress.com

This is a work of fiction. Names, characters, places, and incidents are the products of the author's imagination or are used fictitiously. Any resemblance to actual events, locales, or persons, living or dead, is entirely coincidental.

Portions of this novel first appeared in *ImageOutWrite*, *Hinchas De Poesia*, *Chroma*, *Glitterwolf*, *Best Gay Stories 2017*, and *Velvet Mafia*, and in the author's collection *The Island of No Secrets and Other Stories*.

The novel's title is taken from "Last Letter," a poem by Tim Dlugos.

Paperback Edition
10 9 8 7 6 5 4 3 2 1
Printed in the United States of America

ISBN: 978-0-9708310-4-0
Library of Congress Control Number: 2019954234

Cover design by Tom Schmidt
Front and back photography by Dot
Author photo by Chan Chao

for David,
whose belief in my work made this book possible

CONTENTS

Part I

1962

Part II

Four Years Later

Always There
by Leaving

Part I

1962

CHAPTER 1

PAUL CREEPS OUT his bedroom and to the kitchen window to see who's making noise. It's after midnight. Three figures loiter in the narrow alley below. A woman and two men. Her shiny blue dress covers her shapely body except for her breasts, which she's taken out and caresses. Her ashen skin reflects the naked, incandescent light above.

She sits on a metal garbage can. It screeches under her weight. She starts to slide off but her companions set her right.

"There's one for each of you," she slurs in a gravelly voice. Similar to the words that woke Paul when she barked them louder. Both men, one bone thin and the other stocky, begin to fondle her. They use endearments to draw her back into the dingy neighborhood men's club on the first floor, officially closed for the night.

"Drive me the hell home," she says. A sudden change of heart?

"Sure, Caroline, sure." The bony guy leans forward, kissing a breast. The other one watches as he relights his stogie. He twirls it with plump fingers to make an even burn.

The gesture angers Paul more than anything he's seen or

heard. He grabs a small cup and fills it with water. He checks the building next door for potential witnesses. He holds his arm far out to avoid telltale dripping on the outside wall. In one sharp move he upends the cup and withdraws his arm.

"My fucking head," Caroline yells. "Son of a bitch." She takes a lazy swing at the bony guy as if it were his fault.

The men whisper curses as they search the dark windows above. They get the complaining woman to her feet, try to lure her back inside with the promise of more drink.

"Thought you guys couldn't serve me no more. You said it was too late."

"And so it is," the stocky guy says. "But who's gonna tell?"

Paul's tired of massaging his mother's calves. He has breakfast to eat before he walks the city streets to school, where he's starting seventh grade.

"You'll make me late my first day."

"Five minutes more," she says. "Those were nasty cramps."

He frees one hand for the ashtray, snuffs a smoldering cigarette she lit and then forgot. The smoke makes him dizzy. He watches the clock as he works resistant flesh. The mattress wheezes. Or is it Lenora?

"You'd feel a lot better if you got up and walked," he says.

"Five more minutes."

"You said that seven ago."

"I must've meant twelve."

"But I'm really hungry. And I'm running out of time."

Lenora rolls over and looks at him like he's stupid. "Well then, why don't you go and make something?"

He watches from behind the smudged window of a hallway door. About forty kids on the other side loiter in front of the classroom, unaccountably locked. They sound more like a hundred than forty. Their shrill young voices collide along beige-tiled walls.

One kid reviews the disorderly crowd like a drill sergeant. He smacks a red cap against his thigh as if it were a riding crop. A frown mars his handsome, angular face. He seems on the prowl for vulnerable prey. His name's Hal. Paul heard the name yelled like a chant last year during recess. Some kids grabbed the boy's cap off his head. They teased him for having large bald spots all over his scalp. Hal's hair must've grown back over the summer. Now it's a helmet of brown, thick waves. He wears it longer than any other guy Paul's seen.

A harried-looking teacher appears at the back staircase, keys in hand. She seems the no-nonsense type, has a booming voice. Her order for quiet doesn't need repeating. Kids funnel into the room, eager to claim whole sections of chairs for themselves and their friends. All except Hal. He lingers behind as the line diminishes.

Paul's determined to keep a good distance from everyone. His homeroom period went okay enough. He wants his good luck to hold, wants to get through his first class without incident. He opens the hallway door. A strong draft from behind conveys his gamy smell towards the classroom. He sees Hal pivot like a surprised animal, sees the furious brown gaze that judges his unkempt blond hair and sleepy blue eyes. The wrinkled plaid shirt with missing buttons. Paul knows it's no use. Time to deal. His classroom's isolated. The only one between the back staircase and the hall where he stood waiting. Even worse, the teacher's made a big mistake. She's led her students into the room instead of waiting to assure no stragglers remain.

Like two boys about to rumble.

"What're you doing in my class fish boy?" Hal says once the class door shuts. "You stink like a rotten fish. No one wants you here." He blocks Paul's way, makes him walk back to the hall's end. A wicked grin distorts his face. He puts on his cap. Its bill forms a dark shadow, like a narrow mask, along his eyes and nose. He gets closer to Paul, bouncing on his toes like a boxer. "You stink so much you must live in a sewer."

Paul can't allow such an insult the first day of school. If he does the other boy'll make the coming year a misery.

"I bet you know all about living in a sewer," he says.

And the two reach out to each other with fists and feet. Most of their efforts die in the air. They try grabbing each other to no avail, then draw back to a safe distance. His frustration mounting, Paul lunges in close. He clamps onto Hal's cap and pulls it off by the bill, along with a few brown hairs.

"You're good as dead now." Hal's face puffs in fury. He frees his cap and swats it at Paul. The back snap stings as it lands repeatedly on tender, fair skin. Red marks form along one cheek. Paul reaches for the other's face with his fist. He makes a solid connection that stops the action cold.

"Look what you made me do," he says.

Hal presses two fingers against his nose. He strides to class as the bell sounds. Paul counts the steps. He follows after six in case the retreat's a trick. He gets inside before the ringing stops and takes the last available chair. It's in a back corner. And it's right next to Hal, who's plugged his bloodied nostril with a spitball.

Halfway into the class, the injured boy works his pencil fast over lined notepaper. Paul can see it's a drawing but can't make it out. Meanwhile the teacher rants about JFK's failed invasion of Cuba last year. Her tone grows ominous as she lists the possible consequences.

A flash of yellow appears on his desk.

Is the note really there? His lips move as he reads the neat blue script again and again:

There are small ships,

There are big ships,

   But the best ship is friendship.

9

The drawing above the poem. It's a boat. One with the name Prince Hal written on its sail. The vessel points downward into rippling water. Paul's name floats on the surface in jagged, wavy letters. He looks over to the next row. Morning light glistens along Hal's profile. His skin glows the palest copper. Paul scribbles a reply on the note. In the water—near the sailboat—he sketches a drowning stick figure. The word HELP! fills a cartoon bubble. The paper hisses as he slides it along the other boy's desk. He watches Hal examine the altered drawing.

Neither boy notices the teacher as she makes her way down the aisle to look at, then confiscate, the message without interrupting her lecture.

"I got to use the bathroom." Hal points at his injured nose. "Think I blew it too hard."

All the soap dispensers in the boy's john contain pliant cartridges of thick, green liquid. Once they go empty, they'll pretty much stay that way until the new year.

Hal yanks at one of the plastic dispensers. After much effort the thin feeder tube slips from the bottom slot. He loops the tube into a tight knot. He rinses off any escaped soap, and dries the emerald container with brown paper towels before slipping it into the pocket of his baggy jeans.

"Quit your griping," he tells the other boy, who lags behind. "It ain't much further."

Paul's never gone this far into Branch Brook Park before. He gets lost too easily. And he's suspicious again that the boy who fought him, then seemed to befriend him, might reverse himself in this rocky, secluded area thick with old trees and rampant bushes. He knows isolation can bring out the worst in people. "We've been walking a long time."

"So what?" Hal says. "Like I told you at school, it'll be an adventure. At least for you. I do it anytime I want. My brother used to come too."

"Does he look like you? Maybe I've seen him in school."

"He's more like you—minus the smell."

"Like me?" Paul finds it hard to remember his face. His real face. The last time he could see it clearly in a mirror and recognize his own reflection. All summer long he imagined he was a Chinese prince, the one he saw in a televised story about a nightingale, a mechanical songbird and a selfish emperor. The prince had long black hair and onyx, almond-shaped eyes. He was tall and well-educated. Nothing like Paul. As long as he ignored his body, erased the image of his own face, he remained that far away young man. He could brush his teeth as long as he gazed at nothing in particular. But whenever he washed, had to consider his own skin, the princely facade would dissolve, making his choice clear.

"You think we walked far already?" Hal says. "This

11

ain't nothing. Me and Richie used to hike down to the lake. He liked to watch the fat ducks mess around in the water. They calmed him down, at least for a while." His face clouds, like he's remembered something sad.

"I heard your brother got put away somewhere," Paul says. "Is that true?"

"Here it is," Hal says as if he wasn't asked about Ritchie.

The steep embankment in this hilly area is much lower. About seven feet. Lost in his thoughts Paul failed to hear the water sing along its rocky bottom. "It's a creek," he says.

"No it ain't, it's a river. Just gets small and low around here."

"What're we supposed to do with it?"

"Horse around and other stuff."

"What other stuff?"

Hal doesn't answer. His smirk hardly reassures.

"Look at that." He points below to a wide, flat rock. It hugs the embankment wall like a small peninsula. "All we got to do is hang from the edge and land on that slab. We'll undress down there."

More than ever Paul wishes he could find his way back alone. What's he gotten himself into? He gazes at the rock. The descent seems impossibly far. "How do we get back up?"

"We spread our wings and fly. How do you figure?"

Paul stares blankly at his companion.

"We high-jump," Hal says. "Then we grab onto the

ledge and lift ourselves over. Do I got to draw you another picture?"

"I don't know." Paul needs time to think. This walk in the woods could be an elaborate setup for a practical joke or worse. Maybe Hal's older brother's in on it. Maybe the kid's not put away anymore. He might be lurking close by, waiting to do whatever they have planned.

"Where's your brother now?" he says.

Hal looks angry. Like he did when they fought in the school hallway. He sits atop the embankment, kicks his legs in the air. "Yahoo, Mountain Dew-w-w-w-w-w." Like a wiry animal he lands onto the rock. He removes his red cap, his black-top sneakers and socks. "Go find your way back on your own, you stinky fish-boy mother-fucker. I'm through with you for good."

The words "for good" sound worse to Paul than "put away." More final. "Okay, okay, I'm sorry. Can I come down now?"

"Do what you like," Hal says after a suspenseful moment. Paul sits at the ledge of the embankment and lets his legs dangle. Hal grabs them tight and helps the awkward boy down. "You stink even worse close up. Sooner you get in the better off we'll both be."

It's awkward for Paul, the undressing. What does he look like? What does Hal look like? He strips quickly, following the other boy's example, wishing he really was that handsome Chinese prince. He notices for the first time the

13

gray streaks that line his calves. How they darken to black between the toes. Though deeply embarrassed he can't help meeting the other boy's gaze. He expects to see scorn, revulsion. He finds neither.

"Man you're slow," Hal says matter-of-factly. He strides into the river that's bright with sunlight and stenciled with the shade of leafy trees. His shapely calves cut through water like the prow of a boat. "Jesus Christ it's cold in here."

Paul backs away from the water's edge. His slender naked body turns rigid.

"You better get in," Hal says, "or I swear you're on your own."

Paul inhales loudly and sinks both feet into the gently flowing water that reaches a little above his knees. The smooth, mossy rocks are slippery. He loses his balance, falls backwards with a stinging, wet wallop. "Keep your mouth shut," he hears before his ears fill. "You ain't supposed to drink the stuff," he's told when he surfaces. "It could make you sick."

He watches the other boy tread back to the rock.

"Almost forgot the fun part." Hal digs into his jeans pocket and pulls out the vial of emerald soap pilfered from school. A jagged pen knife reopens the knotted feeder. Shimmering green oozes out until square-tipped fingers stop the flow.

"What's that for?" Paul asks. No answer comes. His companion's playful, shifty smile could mean anything. He braces for the worst. It's a big relief to see the green liquid turn into a jade lather.

"What'd you think it was?" Hal says. "Something to hurt you with? You're such a dumbbell, man. Can't you tell when a guy's being…" He doesn't finish explaining. He sounds pissed, disappointed. "Come here, Stinky Paulie. You need a good washing a lot more than me."

Paul pretends he's making a big concession, but he can't wait to get closer. He falls on his ass against the smooth stones. They yield in their mushy bed. His companion sits nearby. Both of them nearly chest high in chilly, shimmering water, its mild flow kept safely in check by a rocky sluice covered in moss.

"You're a clumsy fuck," Hal says. "Come on now. Cup your hands for me. Make like a monkey and do what I do."

"I know how to wash."

"Could've fooled me."

A green worm of soap wiggles out the vial's opening. It forms a fluid jewel in Paul's waiting hands.

Hal squirts some soap over his own wet head, rests the container on the broad, flat stone. He shampoos with delicate strokes.

Paul wonders if the boy might be worried about all that wavy brown hair falling out again. He mimics his companion. The slow, deliberate movements help him remember what it's like to touch himself and really feel it. Fingers roam his round head. They comb through straw-blond hair darkened by water. My own hair, he thinks, as if it were a new sensation.

"I'm going submarine!" Hal squeezes his nose and falls backward. Soap bubbles crackle atop the surface. He rises from the wet. "Now for you."

He jumps on the other boy and plunges his head to the bottom.

"Too rough." Paul sputters, gasping for air. He doesn't make a big deal of it when he sees Hal stroke himself with soapy hands, so at ease in his body. The drenched skin has the luster of polished brass. As if it never mattered Paul sheds his obsession to be a Chinese prince for another, equally impossible transformation. He mimics the other boy's every move. Washes himself thoroughly, imagining the foam can turn his pale skin honey-colored, mold his torso into a lean, chiseled column, like the one before him.

"Tell me about Richie," he says in a quiet voice. "Why'd your brother have to go away?" He remembers hearing some neighborhood gossip half listened to, and quickly lost in the rolling jumble of his mind.

"Sit your ass down." Hal slaps the water, his face contorted. "No, right here."

Too close for Paul, but he obliges. He can't help gazing at the other boy's small, upturned nose—the bold cheeks and widening chin. He wants to touch that face, examine the maturing planes. Make them his own somehow. A mask that never comes off.

16

"Me and Richie robbed a couple old fucks last year," Hal says. "Some guy and his wife. It was in their house late at night. Richie snuck in through a back window and I played look-out on the porch."

"What'd he take?"

"What do you think? He took money. He saw the old prick walking home from the bank the day before."

"So it was your brother's idea?"

"Yeah. And it was Richie's idea to beat the shit out of them too. Something about those decrepit old people made him crazy. He took off his belt and let 'em have it. The old guy more."

Paul's not sure he wants to know but asks anyway. "What'd *you* do?" He holds his breath, waits for an answer.

"I was outside like I told you. Only found out what Richie did after the cops nabbed him. He never ratted I was there." Hal seems proud of his brother's loyalty. He grabs a fallen leaf, twirls it between his fingers.

"Are they okay now?" Paul says.

"Who?"

"The old couple."

Hal chops at the water as if he were trying to hurt it.

"Those two shit bags landed my brother in reform school. Last month he went AWOL. Ain't heard boo from him since. Maybe he should've killed those old creeps to keep them quiet. What good're they anyway?"

His voice sounds distant, eerie, as if it were coming

from a place outside his body. He gets on his knees and leans in closer to Paul. "I think Richie beat them up because they stank like you do. Like you used to. Maybe I ought to kill you. Drown you now so you can die clean. Hold you under until your eyes roll up in your dumb head. Nobody'd ever know." He wraps his large hands on the other boy's shoulders. "I always wanted to kill someone to see what it feels like."

Paul's almost certain the kid's only being a jerk. But he's rattled by the way Hal looks at him as if he were someone else. "Quit trying to scare me," he says.

"Who's trying?"

"People'd find out."

"No they wouldn't. And who'd give a fuck about a stink bomb like you?"

"Lay off me." With his forearms Paul breaks the strong grip on his shoulders and jumps to his feet. He almost falls on top of the other boy. "You ever think you might lose if you tried? Remember who got the bloody nose at school. I can get plenty angry too. I can hate people. Lots of people." In a froth of water, he strides back and forth—a white streak in the dappled sunlight—inches from Hal, who sags so far down he looks shrunken. A harmless kid again. Harmless and sad.

Paul sits beside him as if there was never any threat. He gazes at the long channel of water ahead. Maybe getting drowned wouldn't be so bad. He heard somewhere it's like going to sleep but never getting up again. Or was that freezing to death? "What happened all of a sudden?" he says. "We were having fun. It felt like fun." He recalls the drawing and the poem Hal gave him in school, where the two sat side by side. "I thought we were friends."

"Who'd want to be friends with you?" But Hal inches closer, leans against his companion. "We better get going." Yet he doesn't stir. Neither does Paul. He feels safe in the chilly, secluded water. Safe with himself and Hal, shoulder-to-shoulder. A single island.

"You ain't putting those on again," Hal says when Paul reaches for his underwear.

"Why not?"

"You just took a bath that's why not."

"But you put yours on."

"Mine ain't filthy, dumbbell."

Paul leaves his shorts and T-shirt and socks on the damp rock. He grabs his sports shirt and pants. "These clean enough for you, or should I walk back with nothing on?"

"I'll go first." Hal squats low and then shoots into the air. His hands grip the embankment ledge. He pulls himself up in one try. "Piece a cake," he brags, gazing down.

Paul takes a jump. And another.

"You got it!" Hal says after the fourth try.

But the dangling boy can't manage to lift himself.

"Try harder."

19

"What do you think I'm doing?" Paul's right cheek is pressed against the sheer embankment. A trail of red ants marches toward him along the pebbly surface. His hot breath scatters them, makes them change course. "Forget it," he says. "I'll need wings."

"Keep holding on. I'll grab your wrists and pull you up." But Hal can't seem to gain enough leverage. "Don't let go or we'll both go down."

"I'm getting tired."

"And this ain't working. We got to get you up some other way. You better drop down for now."

Which Paul does, almost falling backwards into the water.

The two regard each other. Paul sees reproach and throws it back. "If you didn't have to be the first one up, you could've given me a boost at least."

"Shut up," Hal says, "and let a guy think. Maybe if I got a long branch or something."

Paul watches him search the steep ground, explore further away from the water until he's out of sight. The hunt's taking a long time. Too long. Maybe he's been abandoned.

"I got it!" Hal's muffled voice sounds triumphant. He leans over the ledge. "Hi, crybaby."

Paul stares at the half-dressed boy. "Where'd your jeans go?"

"Here they are." Hal drops one pant leg over the ledge. "Grab hold of your end real tight. Then you can walk up the wall while I tow you with the other leg. The way mountain climbers do with ropes."

"That's real smart," Paul says.

"Yeah, I know."

It's disorienting and scary to walk sideways up a slippery wall, but he manages.

The work jeans feel thin as tissue paper in his trembling fists. They seem to stretch like an elastic band pulled to its limit. Was that a tearing sound he heard or only his shoes sliding against rough, pebbled concrete? He stills himself, tries to listen past his heavy breathing. Blood thumps inside his ears like a rubber mallet. He wills his eyes to open, searches the length of Hal's pant leg. The fabric's worn at the crotch.

That's where it could rip. If it should happen.

So focused is he on the fabric, on any ominous sound, he doesn't realize his progress until—

"You're almost there." Hal's voice, strained but clear.

And it's really true. Paul can start believing. Only a little ways more. A little. He shuts his eyes again, imagines himself light as air, weightless as a leaf floating in the river below.

He nears the top, his body still at a right angle with the wall. And then he stalls.

"What's the matter?" His hands are getting tired and numb.

"I could let go right now and let you drop."

Paul studies the hard smile, the unyielding brown eyes as if seeing them for the first time. "I won't beg," he says, without much conviction. "Do what you want."

He wonders how much the fall could hurt, what he'd do alone and injured in this isolated area of the park. It's impossible to look at the other boy's face anymore. He stares instead at the large hands that control his fate. Veins bulge like angry blue rivers about to burst. Knuckles press their bony whiteness against rough skin. Fingers grasp the fabric as if glued to it. But for how long?

Suddenly he's drawn up fast. Three clumsy steps and he's upright, can dig his heels into yielding soil. He's pulled further from the edge. Further still. He crumbles to the ground. His vertigo doesn't subside for what seems like forever. "You okay?" he hears from beside him, the words so near he can feel them. He takes his time sitting up, looks at the straight edge of the embankment to check if the world has stopped spinning.

"I guess so." He takes a deep breath and tries to stand.

Hal's help makes it easier.

They don't speak much during the walk back. Before they exit the park by a different route, they come to an empty recreation area. At its center lay a solid brick structure fronted by two damp sandlots for toddlers. The old building has a separate storage space for maintenance supplies on one side. Lavatories for visitors are on the other.

Paul can't take his eyes off the place. "Wouldn't it be great if we could live here? We could fix up the inside, come here at night when no one's around."

"You want to play house or something?" Hal says.

But Paul can tell the boy's flattered. The closer they come to roads and buildings, the more the park's magic seems to wear off.

"You going to shape up," Hal says, "now that I set you straight?"

"Straight to where?"

"I mean are you going to wash regular, wear clothes that won't smell?"

"What's it to you?"

"Don't want you stinking up my end of the class is all."

They go their separate ways on Mt. Prospect without saying another word. That evening Paul takes a more conventional bath in his own tub. It's a task he resolves to make a habit. His mirror, still a little foggy, holds a surprise. The reflection belongs to him and not the raven-haired, Chinese prince of his children's teleplay. He stands still, expectant, waiting for the image to revert. But it doesn't.

CHAPTER 2

A FEW WEEKS pass before Lenora sees the change in Paul. The tip-off isn't the lack of odor that once surrounded the boy. Her chain-smoker's nose never picked up even that scent. It's the day he asks her how to iron his clothes.

"I don't want to burn them," he tells her. "Or set the house on fire."

His awkward joke makes her laugh. Sometimes she hates the place so much, she wouldn't mind if it burned to the ground.

Usually his not knowing how to do a simple task annoys her. But on this day she finds him disarming, along with his request for help that requires some rare intimacy, other than the occasional massage. Bent over the ironing board, with him beside her, she notices how worn his clothes are. Shirts, pants. Everything. She studies him through the smoke of a dangling cigarette, through her squinting blue eyes. Nothing seems to fit him anymore. He could pass for a hayseed from the Great Depression.

"You need some new ones," she says. "Clothes," in answer to his questioning gaze. "Ask your grandma for the money. And make sure you buy a size larger than whatever fits. You'll grow into everything soon enough."

It strikes her that she'd been doing more laundry recently. Bigger loads full of boy clothes. How'd she miss that?

She watches him follow her technique with the steaming iron. He learns fast. Yet another change in the kid with a mind like a sieve. Is it possible she's done something, however accidental, to cause this improvement? Nothing comes to mind. Though it's hard to remember her day-to-day, other than the plots of TV soap operas. Maybe there's another reason.

"What's Mary been feeding you?" she asks while he irons a tartan-print shirt.

"The same good stuff. Nothing different." Lately Paul's been eating dinner with his grandma two buildings away. Enemy territory for Lenora since her marital separation. She knows Paul favors the arrangement. Her mother-in-law cooks everything to perfection. She can bake her own bread, make her own pasta. Whip up cakes from scratch. Who could compete with that? Who'd want to?

And then there's conversation. Mary probably talks with the boy over their meals, instead of silently munching on burgers or hot dogs while watching TV.

The ironing lesson ends an hour later with another precedent. "You did good," Lenora says. "Go get a chocolate bar and we'll share it." She watches him rummage through the basket of otherwise forbidden treats she keeps by the sofa, close at hand. He lights up when he finds one with almonds. He turns and hazards a smile. A grin rear-ranges her pale, lovely face. But only for a moment.

They meet at a candy store on Summer Avenue, where they watch boys with money to burn work the pinball machine.

On the walk to Paul's home they pass a grocery, a hardware store, a tailor—and more than a few saloons. Each bar has a neon sign hawking "package goods." Most of the small businesses on this street have one or two families living above them in cramped apartments that need serious renovation. Many are young families struggling to get by. It's a street like many others in this blue-collar section of Newark, New Jersey.

A street like Paul's, where Hal takes cover behind the nearest tree, its trunk swollen with disease.

"What's the matter?"

"Those two guys in front of your place," Hal says.

"Which guys?"

"The young ones hanging with those geezers."

"What about them?"

"They gave me and Richie lots of grief once."

"What'd you do?"

"Nothing much."

"Yeah, sure."

"It was only a prank. A little dry ice. We stole a carton off a boxcar down the tracks behind your block. The stuff was all broke to bits. Me and Richie hid behind some tall bushes in the empty lot near the gas station. We waited for people to pass. Slow people. Dumb looking people. When a good target came in reach we'd throw a little ice. We used plastic bags we found as gloves. Then we ducked out of sight."

"A little ice doesn't sound bad."

"I'm talking *dry* ice," Hal says. "It's a chemical or something. Stings like a son of a bitch if you don't get it off your skin quick. Those two guys. They work in the gas station."

"I know them," Paul says. "They're Gussie and Johnny."

"They saw me and Richie nail one of their customers and they chased us. They were fast too. We had to run down the tracks all the way into North Arlington to lose them. Richie stopped long enough to hurl a rock. He almost beaned the redheaded fuck. They yelled they'd kick our butts the next time they saw us."

"How long ago was that?"

"Not long enough."

"They're here for bowling night." Paul should've remembered. His father's probably downstairs in the club with other league members, including the Army buddy he's been rooming with to avoid the embarrassment of moving back in with his mother. So far Paul's kept his friend a secret from Max. Instinct told him to stay mum. He didn't even tell Lenora until he asked if the boy could sleep over.

He timed the request with care, in between his father's scheduled visits, so Lenora wouldn't mention Hal or the sleepover. Not until she met him and took a liking to him. If that's possible.

He doesn't want his friend introduced to Max by a couple guys badmouthing the kid or worse.

"Guess we're stuck for a while," he says. "Let's wait at the candy store."

"Ain't you got another way?"

"Yeah, but the alley to our backstairs hall only has a front entrance. The club fenced up the other end a long time ago."

"Fences are easy to climb."

"Not if there's a mess of barbed wire on top."

"How long we got to wait for them to leave?"

"Until eight or so."

"That's too long."

"No it's not. Unless you want to climb the telephone pole to the back roof."

"That's a great idea, let's do it!"

"I was joking. And only repairmen are allowed to climb that."

"Here's how we play it."

"Play what?"

"You keep a bead on those two clowns. When you give the all clear I'll make a run for the tracks. You follow a little later."

"We should wait at the candy store or do something else. It's really not that long."

"Maybe you're too chicken to hang with," Hal says. "Maybe we should forget about me staying over." He shrugs like he could care less one way or the other.

Paul won't call his bluff. He can tell his buddy's too worked up, eager to launch another pointless challenge for the hell of it.

The boys walk side-by-side on the railroad tracks to see who falls off first. They pass a billboard along the way. It's meant for commuters who live in the suburbs. People with money. Kids often sit on the billboard platform and throw empty liquor bottles at the rails. Bottles they find on weed-filled ground. Bottles left by derelicts who booze it up late at night alone or with a drinking buddy. No one across the way complains. Only a long brick factory stands opposite the tracks. It empties out in the early afternoon.

"That's where my grandma lives," Paul says. "She owns the place." He leads Hal to the fenced-in backyard of a tidy, three-story apartment building where six families dwell. Its fire escape is newly painted deep red.

A German shepherd lounges outside his large clapboard house. He saunters over to the chain-link fence and pokes his snout through a diamond-shaped hole.

Paul strokes the black-and-tan muzzle, and tells his buddy to do the same. Hal keeps his distance.

29

"You shouldn't be scared of old Fritz."

"He's a guard dog, ain't he?"

"And a good one."

"All the more reason then."

"No it isn't. You're with me so he knows you're okay."

Hal's fingertips inch close to the wet, twitching black nose. A rough tongue greets them.

"Boy, he really likes you."

"Must be the French fries I had for dinner." But Hal beams at Fritz like a kid who got his Christmas wish.

"They used to have a garden back here," Paul says. "When my Grandpa was alive."

"What'd they grow?"

"Tomatoes and parsley and zucchini. Other stuff I can't remember. Oh yeah, and basil. They even used to make their own wine. I was real little then. And my uncles and aunts still lived in some of the apartments with their kids.

"Every year grandpa bought boxes of purple grapes off some farm. They'd all go into a big barrel that was hauled out the cellar. It had a press thing on top. Like the clamps we use in shop class. But gigantic. They had to work the press by hand. Take turns going round and round, squeezing the grapes to make juice. It came out a big spout at the bottom. Then they'd put the stuff in smaller barrels and let it change into wine."

The description reminds him of Holy Communion, a ritual he's avoided, along with the requisite confessional, since meeting Hal. "The smell of all those grapes getting pressed made me dizzy. But I liked it. Liked to watch everyone working together."

"They got any left?"

"Any what?"

"Wine, dummy."

"In the cellar. Bottles and bottles of it." He regrets his answer when Hal shows too much interest.

A little further on the boys arrive at their destination.

Paul's building has three stories as well. He lives on the middle floor above the men's club and below another apartment like his. The building once had a backyard too. But years ago, the men's club built a banquet hall addition over that grassy patch. The hall's long, flat roof meets the back of his apartment. Whenever he looks out his bedroom window, or any rear window, all he can see is the tar-papered roof and the red-brick factory across the tracks.

"I don't know about this idea of yours," he says. "Someone might spot us and call the cops." Or his mother. And what about his old man?

"You never know about anything," Hal says. "It's dark out. Who'd want to kill time looking out here?"

"The people upstairs from me do. They can see into Belleville."

Sound logic doesn't stop Hal from wanting to climb the

telephone pole that stands at the back wall of the club's banquet hall.

"Hold this." He tosses Paul a grocery bag with stuff for his sleepover. He climbs the rusty footholds nailed long ago into wood.

"Piece a cake," he says midway up the pole. A short step gets him onto the roof. "What're you waiting for?" He sounds triumphant, as usual. A white bed sheet hanging from a clothesline embraces his lean body. The frayed line extends from the telephone pole to the rear hallway window. The rope is full of laundry. Paul's laundry. Leonora must've forgotten again.

He throws Hal the sleepover bag to catch and climbs the pole. It seems almost every time he and his buddy are together, he has to go up something or jump down onto something he'd rather not. But his ascent inspires a deception Hal should like. If they're not caught first.

"Try and hide in the sheet until I'm up," he says. "I got a smart idea of my own."

The boys follow the laundry to the open hallway window.

Hal has no problem climbing through. Paul does and gets pulled in over the sill.

"That was rough," he says.

"You're here, ain't you? So what's next?"

"We take in the laundry."

"Fuck why?"

"It makes us look good. Gives us a reason for coming the back way."

"Now you're thinking like me."

"Yeah," Paul says, "only you didn't think of it."

Lenora can't imagine who'd be knocking on her back door. The sight of Paul accompanied by an unfamiliar boy gives her a jolt.

"What's all that?" The mound of wash in the laundry basket reaches her son's chin.

"It's ours," he tells her. "Saw it hanging on the line when we were walking along the tracks. Thought me and Hal'd surprise you and take care of it."

"You and Hal?"

"This is him."

"Yeah, it's me all right."

"Remember?" Paul says. "I asked if he could—"

"Of course I do." She opens the door wide to let them in.

Paul glances past his mother. He can see the TV show has Hal sleepy with boredom. It's an old black-and-white movie. A sappy love story where everyone speaks in a foreign accent and wears frilly clothes. Even the men. But it's the only entertainment on offer. Lenora made it clear she wanted company in front of the tube. She kept interrupting the poker game Hal was trying to teach his buddy at the kitchen table.

33

Something about the film has her wound up. She names most every actor in the huge cast, pointing them out. She talks about their lives as if she knows them. Stuff she's read over the years in magazines.

Paul doesn't mind but he knows Hal could care less. He wishes she made more of an effort for company. Instead, she sets her yellow hair in bobby pins and rollers while she watches the movie, just as she does most nights. The blue robe that covers her slender body shows too much thigh when she crosses her legs. Her cigarette smoke clogs the air. She pops her gum frequently. And can't she stop twitching her foot? It makes the whole couch vibrate.

Her habits would bother him less if she hadn't insisted they all sit on the couch, instead of letting him and his buddy each sprawl on a side chair. Now and then he catches her looking him over. Her lips move like she wants to say something. Nothing comes out.

"I'm getting tired," Hal says in a loud voice. He makes a big show of yawning and stretching. His left arm grazes Lenora's shoulder. Her twitching stops; her posture stiffens.

"There's no school tomorrow," she says like it's something no one else knows. "You boys can sleep late as you want."

"I'm used to hitting the sack early 'cause I always get up early. Even on weekends. Ain't that right, Paulie?"

"Yeah, he does." Although Paul has no idea.

The full-sized bed cramps the small, sloping space, what with the bureau and the dresser; their wood stained an anemic blue that matches the faded wallpaper. Still the room has a door Paul can lock, although his mother doesn't know. He found the old eyehole key way back in the kitchen cupboard and kept it secret.

"Man you're lucky," Hal says.

"Why?"

"You got a window that opens to the roof we were on."

"So what?"

"So you can sneak in and out at night any time you want. Long as you're careful."

"I never liked that window. I'm always worried someone can come in, like a robber or murderer."

Hal slips into his side of the bed and tugs on Paul's pajama waist. "You always dress up for bed, scaredy-cat?"

"Yeah. In summer I wear short ones."

"I want to play the game we do in the park."

"Here?"

"Your old lady didn't even say goodnight. She won't bother checking up on us. Besides, that film ain't half over."

Paul listens to the muted voice of a fast-talking guy selling cars. He looks back at Hal, who seems confident of the answer. "We better wait until the ads are over. She might get up for something."

"Okay. And me first."

"You're always first," Paul says in mock complaint. He peels off his clothes and covers himself with the bed sheet. Hal does the same but skips the sheet. He squats on his rear, head cocked toward the door, his silhouette backlit with gray light that seeps through dusty window blinds.

A muffled sound of violins tells them it's time to play.

Later, after it's Paul's turn and both boys are fast asleep, sounds that echo down the tracks disturb his rest. Unfamiliar sounds, high and popping. Sounds the dreaming boy interprets as distant firecrackers exploding all at once.

In the morning he sets two cereal boxes onto the yellow Formica tabletop.

"Which kind you want?"

Hal squints. His eyes are puffy from sleep. He grabs the bigger box. Paul's favorite. There's not enough for them both so the young host settles for second best. Pillows of woven grain tumble into his bowl. Hal grabs the newspaper and pulls out the funnies. Bare florescent tubes above them cast the room in harsh light. But the kitchen'd be too dark and gloomy otherwise.

Paul butters their toast and fills two green mugs almost to the top. He brewed the coffee stronger than usual to suit his buddy. His knowing Hal has made him more attentive to other people, more aware of how to behave around them. He can recall things better too. Even the lessons taught in school, as long as they don't involve too much math. It's as if he can draw upon the other boy's eyes and ears, and every other sense as well. He smiles with gratitude.

And Hal misunderstands. "So I like a lot a sugar in my coffee."

Paul watches the third and final spoonful dissolve in the hot, swirling liquid.

CHAPTER 3

THEIR BREAKFAST IS nearly finished when the boys hear a loud knock. It has a teasing, musical rhythm.

Hal looks at Paul like, What gives?

In slippers and drooping pj's, Paul runs to the front door before the racket awakens his mother. He wants to be out of the apartment without having to deal with her. Who knows what mood she'll be in. How she might treat Hal in the morning, always a dicey time. Maybe it's the newspaper boy wanting to get paid. Or the bread boy. But those annoying, pimple-faced kids always comes later, per Lenora's instructions. And they never make that much noise. Then Paul remembers his parents' last argument, the new agreement ironed out after much shouting.

"Hi Dad."

"Paulie!" Max tussles his son's flaxen mop. In the dark hallway his square face, veiled in a cloud of mentholated smoke, has a spectral quality. A green zipper jacket stretches around his growing paunch.

"Nice knock you got there," Paul tells him.

"Your mother doesn't want me coming in unannounced anymore, even though I pay the bills." Max walks to the sliding double doors of her bedroom just off the parlor.

He's poised to knock, then seems to think better of it. "Let me take a wild guess. Sleeping Beauty ain't up yet, right?"

Paul offers a circular nod that could mean yes or no. He's thinking more of Hal, not sure what to say about him. Where to start.

Max offers a conspiratorial smile. Paul hates when his father pretends to like him, that they're buddies, that Max didn't wish he had another son. One who'd make him feel proud. He knows his old man's been angling to come back home again but getting nowhere.

"Looks like someone's having breakfast." Max rubs a few toast crumbs off his son's cheek. "Think I'll join you. After all, it's Poppa's money."

In the kitchen he sees two place settings of used bowls and mugs and plates. Water flows in the bathroom. "Didn't you say she was sleeping?" He doesn't wait for an answer, raps hard on the bathroom door. "Nice to see you rise'n'shine for a change, darling. Thought I'd come over for a little breakfast with the family. Tell you what happened down the street last night. The whole neighborhood's talking about it."

The bathroom faucets whine and complain as they're shut.

"Been meaning to fix those," he says.

"Then why don't you?" Lenora leans against the kitchen doorway behind him. Her voice sounds hoarse. Her blonde bangs, set in bobby pins, have loosened during the night. Her blue robe covers her thin body like a terrycloth tent.

"Who's in the bathroom, Leo?" Max says.

Lenora looks at her son then her husband. "Paul's friend, I guess."

"Paul's? I didn't know you had any friends. Why didn't you say something before, wise guy? And here I am thinking it was you in there," he tells his wife.

"Big deal, so you're wrong again." Lenora glides past him, makes a beeline for the electric percolator to get a fresh pot going.

Paul's about to explain when the bathroom door opens with a sharp swing. Hal walks out barefoot. He's wearing only a T-shirt and jeans. A pair of worn gray socks dangles from his fist.

"Morning all." He sounds casual, like he didn't hear the family conversation, although he must've.

"This is Hal," Paul tells his grimacing father. "Hal Darvis. He's my friend. He stayed over last night for the first time."

He puts a hand on his buddy's shoulder, mostly to keep Hal from advancing closer to Max with that cocky stride. He's sure his words sound heavy with guilt. Like a full confession about what they did under the covers and in the dark, while Lenora watched TV in the parlor and chain smoked. Maybe he should've said *a* friend instead of *my* friend. Of all the mornings for his father to show up and—

"Do it like you was taught," Max says.

"Do what?"

"What about me?"

"Oh yeah. Sorry." Paul mumbles a feeble introduction.

His father cocks his head, takes a long, critical look adults can get away with when they give a kid the once-over. "So you're Hal Darvis. You got a brother named Richie, ain't that right?"

"Last time I checked." Hal's stance grows wider. He crosses his arms, looking to Paul like a handsome boy soldier at ease, but ready for combat.

"I know the old couple your brother beat up and robbed," Max says. "They're good people. Wonderful people. Their sons are my friends. We grew up together and played in each other's homes." He takes a step closer. "Now those old folks are scared all the time, afraid to go out. They won't open their door to no one but family."

Hal looks down at his feet and then at Paul, who wishes he could pipe in, say his friend had no idea Richie was going to rob someone. But he couldn't manage such a big lie. Not without Max seeing through it.

"You boys want more breakfast?" His mother talks as if there's no tension in the air, like she walked into a room full of laughter. "Why don't I fix us all some bacon and eggs and toast?" She gets down to business, collecting the raw ingredients from the refrigerator, cradling them in her arm.

"I should go," Hal says. "Got stuff to do."

"Stick around," Max tells him. "Growing boys like you

and Paulie need more to eat than cereal. I got something to tell everyone about the neighborhood. Something that'll interest you in particular." He doesn't say why, only gestures for Hal to sit down, steering the boy to a nearby chair. "And put your socks on. No one eats barefoot here."

Hal takes his time complying. He backs up his chair so it drags hard against the worn red linoleum.

"I'll get the table going." Paul removes the dirty dishware and utensils and piles them into the sink. He has to make several trips to the cupboard for clean ones. He takes care not to drop anything, do something clumsy in front of Max.

Lenora turns from the stove for a quick inspection. "Don't forget the juice glasses."

He slowly works his way around the table. He wishes he could switch chairs with his friend, give the boy more distance from his father. Max has the same look of disdain for Hal that he directs at Paul whenever he thinks his son can't see. Only now he doesn't bother hiding it, except for a jagged smile. The opposite of friendly.

"Hal's in the same class as me," Paul says while he gets orange juice from the refrigerator. "We sit next to each other. That's how we became friends."

"You a good student?" Max says. "Do your homework regular?"

"I get my share of Cs and Bs."

Paul envies how his buddy can throw enormous bull with a straight face.

His old man makes a show of being impressed. "Hear that Paulie? The kid gets Cs and Bs. Not Cs and Ds, like someone we know."

"I'm doing much better this year. You'll see when I get my next card. There'll be a lot more Cs. Maybe some Bs."

"Your mom and me don't want you staying behind."

"I won't," Paul says. He resolves to spend more time on his homework, less time goofing around. Anything that'll make his buddy look like a good influence. He folds into his chair next to Hal. "That bacon sure smells great," he says to change the subject. He can't remember when he last saw his mother move around the stove so fast. Already the coffee pot's starting to gurgle. And the frying pan—the one that takes two hands to lift—sizzles and sputters as she removes the strips of meat with a fork and places them on a paper towel to dry.

She seems to be enjoying herself. But he can't tell for sure with her back to him most of the time.

"And what about you, Max?" she says over the hissing, black pan. "Are you going to get better grades too?"

"Me?" He twists his head around to see her. "I thought we were talking about Paulie's schoolwork." He turns back to his son. "Am I missing something here, or is your mother in one of her dreamy moods?"

"It's the end of the month," she says, "and I'm still waiting again. You promised you'd do a lot better. So far, you're getting an F."

43

"Oh that," Max says. "Don't worry, Leo, I got it. Forgot to bring it is all. On account of what happened last night. That's why I came over."

"I can't imagine what kept you from stuffing some bills in your wallet."

"What happened last night?" Paul says. "It have anything to do with firecrackers?" He wants to change the subject again and fast. Doesn't want his parents to have another big money blowup. Hal might get caught in the crossfire.

His old man gives him a funny look.

"I had a dream last night. It seemed real. There were lots of firecrackers going off. Maybe cherry bombs. All at once kind of. And from far away."

"I did too," Hal says although he never mentioned it to Paul.

"You boys weren't exactly dreaming," Max tells them. "There was a big shoot-out down on Broadway at the train station. About half a dozen cop cars surrounded the place. Peanuts told me all about it. His son's on the force. He said there was a big hail of bullets and then nothing. A long stalemate. The cops went back and forth with one of the hoods. They were setting up a surrender deal."

"How many were there?" Paul says.

"Three if you count the girl."

"A girl?" Lenora says suddenly showing interest. "What'd she do?"

"Nothing much. She was the bartering chip. A skirt the

punks could hide behind. Pregnant to boot. If it weren't for her, both those creeps'd be dead instead of only the one."

"A guy got killed?" Paul says.

"Died in the ambulance. Peanuts told me both were wanted for armed robberies. The other one'll get locked up for a long, long time." Max looks directly at Hal. "Death or prison. So much for a life of crime."

"None of this surprises me," Lenora says. "We live on a lousy street in a lousy city that's getting worse every year. What should we expect?"

"There's nothing wrong with this street," Max tells her. "Or the neighborhood. Just some rotten eggs who come in and stink up the place. Ain't that right boys?" And again, he looks only at Hal.

"Well these eggs aren't rotten." Lenora swivels around and shows them the clear glass bowl filled with viscous yellow. "Hope you like them scrambled, Hal, it's too late otherwise."

He looks up and nods, his full lips pressed tight, his olive skin glazed with pink.

She smiles and gives him a wink.

It's a simple gesture, but one that means so much to Paul. He wants to thank her. Tell her how grateful he is if he could. If he knew how. He's not sure why his mother's being so nice. Maybe she really likes Hal, though he suspects she only wants to needle his old man, who's made his feelings about the boy all too clear.

"By the way," Max says. "How's your mother doing? I heard from a couple guys down the club that your father's on another long haul. Must be hard on your mom being left alone so much. Especially at night. I hear she gets real lonely."

Paul watches Hal drop his hands under the table as if he doesn't trust what he might do with them. His eyes grow darker, rounder. "My mom ain't alone, she's got me. I can take care of her good enough."

"Right. She's got you." Max peers at the boy over his glass. He slurps the chilled juice that's even more yellow than the eggs Lenora displayed.

"So what about *your* mom?" Hal says. "How's she doing? Paul's told me a lot about her. What a good cook she is. How she lives in that apartment building by herself."

He says it real friendly, like he wants to be polite. But Paul can tell the words aren't meant that way. He knows without even looking at his old man that something bad has happened. Something he can't fix with another change of subject. Behind his tight smile Hal seems miserable. Defiant. Like he wants to smash a plate on Max's head. A thing Paul, in his alarm, wouldn't put past the impulsive boy.

He reaches for the newspaper he'd tossed onto the cold radiator. "Here you go, Dad." He holds the sports section in front of Max until his father takes it and quits staring at Hal.

"I'd like the funnies again," Hal says. "Think I skipped some of my regulars."

Paul settles on the front section. He tries to focus on a story about a Berlin Wall the Russians are building.

Minutes go by. They're filled with silence, except for Max, who turns the pages like he wants to tear them; and Lenora, who mutters a swear word whenever a drop of grease lands on her hand. Worst of all, Hal looks at the funnies like he's not even reading them.

Maybe the newspaper was a bad idea. Paul searches for something to talk about that'll break the ice a little. He turns to his mother when he comes up empty. She could get a conversation going. But she seems tuned out again, lost in her own thoughts as she goes around the table serving everyone—starting with the fresh, hot coffee that smelled so good a few moments ago.

Almost as one they pick up speed, eat fast, as if the meal is work, as if they're all strangers in a restaurant, stuck sharing the same table, eager to get away.

Hal eats the fastest. Even the stringy bacon he wolfs down. Paul wishes his buddy would look up once so they could at least exchange glances, reassure each other. He worries Hal might blame him for his old man's behavior. Maybe end their budding friendship.

"Guess what?" Lenora says. "I know what we should do today." She sounds happy and excited, as if everyone's been having a good time she's going to make better. "We should take a long ride in the suburbs. Someplace like Nutley or Upper Montclair. Like we used to on Sundays, remember Max?" She gives Hal a big smile. "You come too, of course. We can drive around the neighborhoods, point out our favorite houses. Pretend we live someplace half-way decent instead of . . ." She sighs dramatically and tears into her toast.

Paul knows the drive won't happen. His mother isn't serious. She only wants to aggravate Max with a subject that'll leave him sore, get him wishing he hadn't come and disturbed her sleep, put a crimp in her Saturday morning. A morning that would've gone better without him. Better for everyone.

Again he's at a loss for words. He elbows his sullen friend gently but gets no response. He fakes a loud sneeze into his soggy paper napkin. His parents say God bless you as if it were a competition. A moment later Hal says gesundheit instead and it's enough. More than enough, Paul finds it funny.

CHAPTER 4

"I DON'T KNOW," Paul says, "it sounds risky. You sure you've done it before?"

"Of course I'm sure. I don't live in a daydream like you. Me and Richie worked like a team. We never had no trouble."

"I may daydream a lot, but I know bull when I hear it."

Paul doesn't need to see Hal to know the boy exaggerates, so attuned is he to any change in his friend's inflection no matter how nuanced. If only he could learn to anticipate quicker, somehow get inside his buddy's head. Then he'd have more time to think. Plot a good counter argument on the spot. One that wouldn't lead to a quarrel or a permanent falling-out, always his major fear.

Static on the bad connection fills a long pause. He hears a click. Did Hal hang up? Or is it that nosy stranger who shares the party line?

"Maybe me and Richie had one close call our first try. That was a long time ago."

"If I do it," Paul says, "it'll be *my* first try."

"Yeah, but you'll be with me. I'll show you the ropes beforehand."

"How much?"

"What?"

"How much trouble did you get into your first try?"

"Got away scot-free. Absolutely. Only problem was we could never go back again. Like we cared. It was a crumby little place anyway."

Paul can't help thinking about Richie getting sent to reform school, a forbidden subject to raise since his buddy's encounter with Max. "Let's talk about it more after we meet up."

"I can do this without you," Hal says. "I can do everything without you."

There's a second clicking sound followed by another silence, this time longer. Too long. The static comes in waves. It reminds Paul of bare skin sliding against cold bed sheets that never get warm. "I'm almost sure I want to do it," he says. Close to a yes without being one. Enough to reach the next step, seeing Hal, who seemed excited when he first called. Paul waits for an answer, waits to know if he's still speaking to his friend, the mysterious party line or only himself.

The train station sits on a weedy hill close to where his block meets Broadway. Paul runs his hand along the station's weathered, yellow clapboard. "I found twenty-six." He sees more holes in the wood, but doesn't bother adding them, so bored is he by his own stall tactic. On their way to catch the bus, he made up a story to divert his buddy here, telling Hal he heard a kid brag about finding money around the station. Lots of money. After they exhausted their search for easy cash, Paul suggested counting bullet holes left by the shootout several months ago. He made it a competition to guarantee his buddy's interest.

"Found thirty-seven on my side," Hal says. "I win big time!"

"You win again. What a surprise."

"If you think I'm lying add them up yourself."

"Who said anything about lying?" Paul examines a hole emptied of its deadly contents by a cop seeking evidence, or by a kid hunting for souvenirs. Other holes—empty or not—have been spackled over, dotted with yellow paint. Makes them even easier to spot. All the broken window panes have been replaced. Paul can tell which ones by the fresh caulking that resembles dried toothpaste.

Hal enters the station. He slouches on a long wooden bench in the waiting room. Paul reclines nearby despite the chilly surface. He rests his head close to the other boy. They almost touch. "It'd be great if we could live here, wouldn't it?"

"Playing house again?" Hal says. "Maybe we can sack out with the ghost of that guy the cops knocked off. Ain't you heard this place gets haunted late at night?"

"Only by drunks sleeping it off. I never pegged you for a kid who believed in ghosts."

"I believe in everything bad because anything bad can happen. And how'd you know one way or the other?"

51

"About the drunks or you being superstitious?"

"Don't get wise." Hal lightly squeezes the other boy's nose, and then locks onto it, forcing Paul to sit up for better defense.

"You're such a jerk." He swipes away his buddy's hand.

"You're such a jerk," Hal mimics. "That's what girls always say."

"They're onto something when it comes to you."

"We probably should head downtown."

Hal sounds almost resigned. Much less eager than he was on the phone. Maybe he's had a change of heart. Maybe Paul can alter their afternoon plan if he can gain more time to dream up an interesting alternative. "Why don't we have a snack at the candy store first?"

"I ain't hungry."

"You're always hungry for a snack."

"It's too far."

Paul's home isn't too far. But he can't take his buddy there. Hasn't been able to since that awful breakfast, after which Max ordered him to end the friendship.

Whenever the boys want to fool around like they did the night of Hal's first and only stay-over, they go elsewhere. Sometimes after school's out they manage to sneak up to the building's top floor. Paul plays lookout in the empty hallway. Hal uses his pen knife to jimmy the faulty lock on the girls' Home Ec room. Once inside they make a beeline for the spacious pantry. But most times they freeze their butts off behind some bushes in the park. Paul still hasn't been invited to his buddy's home. Not even to meet up there. And he hasn't tried to wheedle an invitation, no matter how often his curiosity's tempted him.

"I used to come here before nightfall," he says. "The year I started first grade. I liked to think the station was all mine. That there'd be people and even talking animals coming to see me. Coming on the train."

"Bet you had a long wait." Hal takes his turn stretching out on the bench. He crosses his legs at the ankles.

"Sometimes there'd be a guy hanging out," Paul says. "He'd be drinking cheap wine like Tiger Rose. You've seen the label. It's got an angry tiger jumping out a big red flower. Green leaves all around. Real pretty."

"Pretty?" Hal says.

"Yeah, I said pretty. I took an empty bottle home with me one night, so I could look at it whenever I wanted. Like a picture on a wall. My mom spotted the bottle and threw it out. Told me I'd get sick from touching stuff bums slobbered over."

"You hear that?" Hal crouches low, turns an ear to the ceiling.

"What?"

"Upstairs. The floor creaked."

"You're trying to psyche me out. I didn't hear a thing."

"Shut up and you will."

The boys listen hard. They gaze at the tin ceiling,

painted the same caterpillar green as the walls. Whoever's upstairs can't be a commuter. Trains don't stop at the station on weekends anymore. Nor is there a clerk to sell tickets no matter the day. Those commuters who do show up during the workweek have to pay on the train. Besides, Hal checked the upstairs door twice already. He even tried to pick the new lock, which proved well beyond his skill.

"It's probably a janitor," he says. "Or some other railroad clown."

Reserved for "Official Use Only," the second floor stays bolted during off hours. But oversight of the building is haphazard at best; otherwise the entire station, including the waiting room, would be closed until early Monday for the morning commute.

"You want to leave?" Paul says.

"I ain't scared. But I bet you are."

"Who said you were? And no, I'm not." Although he is. Paul should've known his buddy would turn a simple question into another meaningless dare.

Yet both boys jump at the sound of clumsy feet on wooden stairs, and the clanking noise that echoes in the narrow hallway like ominous bells. Muffled curses melt into plaintive sobs. The protracted descent suggests that someone—or something—large and cumbersome is on the move. Despite his bragging claim of disbelief, each step reminds Paul of the first spirit in "A Christmas Carol," the one that emerges shackled in chains with enormous locks.

"I wonder how chains on a ghost can weigh anything?" he whispers. "Or make a noise? Shouldn't they be light as air? Shouldn't the ghost just slip away from them?"

"What the fuck are you talking about?" Hal backs away towards the exit and yanks his friend with him.

"I'm talking about the movie we saw at assembly. That Jacob Marley guy."

"Put a lid on it so I can hear. And don't move a muscle."

His having to remain still instantly makes Paul itchy. The sensation starts along his left ear. It pops up on the tip of his sharp nose. Blossoms along his slender neck. He scratches himself as if he had a major case of poison ivy. "The noise's stopped," he says.

"No kidding. Am I deaf?"

But the eerie sounds get replaced by those of creaking hinges and heavy breathing. Finger by finger, like the legs of a slinking crab, a gnarled hand grabs the door's edge and pushes it outward.

"Whew! Those stairs are too steep for an old-timer like me." The short, hunched man gulps for air. He squints at the boys. His dull gray eyes bulge from their sockets above a beaky nose festooned with angry veins. His weaving stance reminds Paul of a toy gyroscope that wobbles soon after it's spun. He hopes the spindly guy won't collapse like that gadget.

"Hi there fellas," the grizzled man says once he's caught his breath. His serpentine wave recalls the sloppy benedic-

55

tion of a bored priest. His etched skin hangs around his neck like rubbery tree bark. It jiggles when he speaks.

"So tell me, are you white or are you Irish?"

"I don't get you." There's a hard note in Hal's voice, like he's been insulted.

"Never mind. It's an old joke for a different time. A much better time if you ask me."

"No one's asking." Hal sidles to his left and cranes his neck. "What you got hiding behind your back?"

The old man moves forward. The door behind him locks shut.

Hal retreats, dragging Paul with him.

"You've nothing to fear." The man's nearly toothless grin lines his blotched face like a dense highway map.

"No one's scared of you," Hal says.

"Now that we've cleared that up, might one of you boys help me out of this awkward predicament?" The man brings his arm forward. The action sets off loud clanging.

"Shit. They're just booze bottles." Hal seems disappointed.

"Indeed they are. And the miserly source of my latest disgrace. Two of my poor fingers are imprisoned within—see?" The man's index finger has a small, blue-tinted bottle dangling from it. A round, amber number hangs on his ring finger. "It's my knuckles. Must've swelled up on me when I fell asleep with my fingers in the pot as it were. There's a good lesson for you, boys. Never put yourselves in the arms of Morpheus with your digits where they don't belong."

"Morpheus?" Hal says. "Is he upstairs?"

"More like downstairs, deep in the darkest underworld where he reigns. He's the Roman god of sleep you know."

"Guess I don't."

"I do," Paul says. "I got a picture book on ancient mythology from the library."

"Good for you," Hal says. "What I want to know is how'd this guy get upstairs? That lock's a bitch."

The old man taps the side of his nose. "I've an in with the custodian who tends the station. If I happen to be visiting the neighborhood while he's on duty, I help the kindly gent clean. In exchange for modest compensation. A place to rest my weary head in safety. It's all on the q.t., of course." He nods stiffly at the ceiling. "There's nothing of value up there, son, if that's what you want to know. The railroad's cleared out the place except for the conveniences. Thank goodness. But soon they'll cut off the water. Rip out the pipes for scrap. And we all know what that means."

"If I do," Hal says, "I must've forgot."

"Demolishment," the man whispers as if referring to something vile. The word seems to deflate his spare body. He sinks onto a bench. The bottles dangling from his hand clang until they settle. "Demolishment," he repeats. "The bane of modern civilization."

"You mean the station'll get torn down?" Paul says. "But they've been patching it up."

The man shrugs. "It's called Progress. And the true cause of my ruination."

"You ain't making sense," Hal says. "Are you still drunk? Never mind. We don't care. We got someplace else to be."

"Don't let me keep you."

"You won't."

"It's only that I'd appreciate an assist first."

"No handouts to bums," Hal says, as if stating official policy

The man winces at the description. "Who's referring to money? Although I'd welcome a donation for some nectar of the gods. To relieve my discomfort." He rattles the bottles.

"You got a free hand. Pull them off yourself."

"I've tried, but it hurts too much and I defer. It's like having to give myself a shot."

"Bet you give yourself plenty of those."

"I mean an injection. The kind a doctor gives."

"So go see one."

"Let me try," Paul says. "I got my finger stuck in a bottle more than once." He kneels at the bench, inspects the old man's hand. The thin pale skin reminds him of a soggy communion wafer. "I have to twist it round and round while I pull. The bottle I mean. All you have to do is hold your finger in place above the rim, like this."

He starts slow and easy once the old man's ready. The twisting part goes well enough, but the pulling's a different matter. "You got some pretty big knuckles."

"It's my arthritis. Had it for years—Jesus, Mary and Joseph!"

"The kid's only started," Hal says, "and already you're a crybaby."

"No," Paul says, "it's my fault. My elbow slipped off the bench while I was pulling." He looks up to show his sincerity and gets a pat on the head.

"You're doing fine." The man's face is clammy. He sounds winded again. "We make a great team you and me. Like Leon and Les."

"Who're they?" Paul asks, more to keep the guy's mind occupied than from curiosity.

"I'm one of them."

"Which one?"

"Leon McGuire, at your service—Ouch!"

Paul holds up the small blue bottle in triumph. "One down and one to go."

"Take special care with this one. There's a touch more libation inside."

"More what?"

Leon holds the bottle at an angle. "See the pale amber collect in that corner?"

Paul sees only a couple tablespoon's worth. Nothing to fuss over. But he assures the man he'll take extra care. Leon's index finger has a more damaged joint to work past. The boy has to finesse his moves. Advance and retreat. He digs into his pocket, sacrifices his new stick of lip balm, using its waxy contents as a lubricant. He takes his time. More time than his buddy has patience for, a thing made clear by much grumbling and long sighs.

"I'm counting to ten," Hal says. "You got till then."

"Count slow," Leon tells him.

"You wish."

"How's about a story to pass the time while the young doctor here administers?"

Hal stops rapping his youthful, healthy knuckles on the other bench. "What kind of story?"

"One filled with risqué jokes and songs. Plenty of bawdy dancing."

"What does risqué mean?" Paul says although he has a pretty good idea. "And bawdy?"

"They mean sexy. In a suggestive way, more or less. Very tongue-in-cheek. But are you lads old enough?"

"You bet we are," Hal says much to Paul's relief. It's the first time his buddy's been halfway nice to the poor guy, this Leon, who smells like his grandfather's old winepress up close, whose blue coat and baggy gray pants are covered in soot. He recalls how Hal kept calling him "Stinky Paulie" their first day of school. How they fought. How they still fight sometimes over nothing. Forgetting himself he gives the bottle a serious yank. One that sets Leon wailing.

And Paul apologizing.

Meanwhile Hal wraps his hands around his mouth, lets out a howl that ends in a Tarzan yodel.

The long, derisive yell stuns Leon to silence. "Much obliged for the sympathy."

"Glad to help."

"How about that story?" Paul says. "The risky one?"

"Ris*qué*," Leon corrects. "It's coming, but first things first. Whom do I have the pleasure of addressing?"

Paul introduces himself and then Hal when his buddy doesn't volunteer.

"To your health." Leon raises the bottle over his large shiny head. He sucks on the lip and then releases it. His bowed tongue hovers below, waiting to catch the last drop. His body quivers. His face turns bright scarlet, the way actors do in films when they've drunk poison. He stares angrily at the bottle. "Better than nothing, I suppose. The tiny spark that turns the rusty engine."

"So get going, Sparky," Hal says. "You owe us a story."

"Us?" Paul says. "I don't remember you lifting a finger."

"Here's one." Hal shoots him the bird.

"Boys, boys, let old Leon think." He purses his thin, peeling lips, makes a big show of stroking his temple. It has a pulsating blue vein that looks about to pop. "There's so much, where shall I start?"

"How about the beginning?" Paul says.

"Smart boy!" Leon doffs an imaginary hat.

"You think he's smart? You should talk to his teachers."

"Shut up," Paul says.

61

"You shut up."

"A tit serenader." Leon's eyes turn watery, like they're melting in their sockets. His shaky hands fly in the air.

His words get instant attention.

"A who?" Paul says.

"That's what we young tenors were called in burlesque during its heyday. Tit serenaders."

"Burlesque," Paul says. "That's show business."

"With a capital *S*. The real thing. Live on stage. Not like those crap movies, you should pardon the expression."

"I like movies."

"Me too," Hal says. "Especially the scary one's where the monster comes from behind." He grabs Paul in a head-lock, gives him a noogie.

"Get off me, creep." Paul frees himself with a poke to his buddy's middle. "Why were you called a tit serenader? Is it because all you singers were short?"

"My size had nothing to do with it." Leon seems put out. "A tit serenader crooned his tune while a stripper did her routine. The flirtatious gamine would do a slow peel— teasing the crowd into a frenzy—while the singer warbled a ditty into a microphone offstage. The more sentimental the better. Songs like 'Sweetheart of Sigma Chi' and 'Mother Machree.' It was meant to be ironic, you see."

"What's that?" Paul says.

"Funny, in a mocking way. Something your charming pal has a talent for."

"So why'd you have to sing offstage?" Hal says. "Because you stank?"

"Hey!" Paul says.

"No need to object," Leon tells him. "The boy's right. Most of us tenors weren't all that good. We got hired because we came cheap. We also doubled as announcers for the acts. Played straight men for the second-rate comics. The first-rate ones as well when their partners showed up too drunk. In the glory days we worked an eighty-hour week. But I never minded."

"Tell us some jokes then," Hal says. "Short ones we can remember."

"They're the only kind I *can* remember. I've become a liver-head in my dotage. But I'm game." Leon rises from the bench wincing all the way. He slides his toes along the floor. "My ersatz theater—that means fake." He nods at Paul, who claps hard, while Hal crosses his arms.

The old man bows, holding his left hip on the upswing. "Picture, if you will, a man dressed in baggy pants. A crooked beat-up hat. A gaudy wide tie that never was in style. Now he's the top banana. The comic. Meanwhile there'd be me, your typical straight man. Looking dapper. A regular sharpie. Once again we have theatrical contrast. Get the picture?"

"I can see it like I'm there," Paul says.

"What about the jokes?" Hal says.

Leon raises a crooked finger. "So I'm on stage, playing

the straight man. The comic comes barreling up to me and says, 'I'm named after both my parents, you know. My father's name is Ferdinand. And my mother's name is Liza.'

"'So what's your name then?'" I ask.

"'Why it's Ferdiliza!'"

Both boys remain silent, awaiting the punch line until they realize from Leon's eager expression they've just heard it.

"I don't get it," Hal says.

"I think he means fertili*zer*," Paul tells him. "That smelly stuff they put on the school grounds."

"That joke stinks even more," Hal says.

Leon's spare form wilts under the criticism "That was only a warm up. Here's another. And this time we'll have some audience participation, shall we? Help you boys get into the spirit of the thing. Now Paul, after I say my first line, you say the word 'pale?' like it's a great big question. I'll be the comic."

"You want me to stand?"

"Why not? Come join me on stage. Share the spotlight. You can be Les. He was my partner a couple years when we tried to get a comedy act on its legs. During the Depression, it was. We'd have been a hit too if we had top banana shtick, and Les didn't go and—"

"How about the damn joke," Hal says.

Leon twitches all over, like he's aching to do something but can't. "So I'm in a saloon," he says. "I'm dressed in my

Sunday best. I walk over to our young barkeep over here and say, 'I'll have a ginger ale my good man'."

"P-a-l-e?" Paul says, stressing the inflection for all it's worth.

"No," Leon says, "just put it in a glass."

"That's a good one," Paul says, though he thinks it corny as the first.

"Strike two," Hal shouts.

"Let's go for broke," Leon tells them. "Here's one for you."

"I ain't standing," Hal says.

"No never mind." Leon makes a gnarly fist. "Pretend I'm holding a mirror by its long handle. Will you do that much?"

"Okay."

"As I stare into the looking glass, I'll start whining and complaining."

"That should be easy for you."

"Once I'm done you ask me, 'What's the matter?' You're such a clever lad, I'm sure you'll figure out your next line all by yourself."

"I'm sure too," Hal says.

Leon holds the imaginary mirror to his face. His eyes bulge even further. His mouth drops. He lets out a sigh that turns into a whimper that builds into a full-blown cry. "Oh no," he says. "It can't be! This is terrible! Horrendous! I simply can*not* stand it!" He looks down at Hal and nods.

"What's the matter?" Hal says like he's bored.

"What's the matter you say? Take a gander at this mirror and tell me what you see." Leon holds the phantom glass before the boy.

"I see myself."

"Oh thank God," Leon says. "For a while there I thought it was me."

"Now that one's really funny," Paul says. "Isn't it?"

But Hal's not laughing. Instead he glowers as if suspicious the joke might be an insult, something Paul's not sure of as well, considering Leon's sly, satisfied expression. "Tell us about the strippers," he says to change the subject and get a firsthand account of the "risqué." He likes the fancy, old-fashioned way Leon talks. He could listen to the geezer for hours.

"I was wondering when you'd get around to asking." Leon taps his finger against his florid nose again. "Boys will be boys."

"Were they good dancers, the strippers? Did they wear pretty outfits?"

"Interesting questions. I'd've thought you'd want to know if the girls were pretty."

Paul gets flustered without knowing why.

"Were they?" Hal says.

"Gorgeous," Leon tells him. "Sublime. Especially under those rose-amber lights that made their flesh luminescent. Smoothed out the rough edges. And what a show the best of them put on. So imaginative."

"Like what?" Paul says. "What'd they do besides take off their clothes and dance around?"

"The art was in *how* they stripped. They each had their own socko gimmick. The ones with top billing anyway. Take Yvette Dare. A raven-haired goddess if ever there was. And I've seen plenty. She had this routine where she'd come on stage in a feathered bra and sarong. The feathers were made to peel off one by one. But her big trick was the two enormous parrots she brought with her. There'd she'd be, bumping and grinding to the wild beat of African drums. Meanwhile the trained parrots would undress her with their formidable beaks. Right down to her G-string and pasties."

Leon grinds as best he can to the imagined sound of exotic drums. His gaunt body vibrates with energy. His long, thick fingernails effectively represent beaks as he pantomimes a costume detaching bit by bit. "Those clever birds," he says, "A flaming miracle they were. Never left a scratch on Yvette's luscious flesh, which she covered in brown makeup to give her that native-girl look."

"Sure wish I could see that," Paul says. "Don't you?"

"I might give it a shot," Hal says.

That's praise enough for Paul. "Tell us another?"

"How about Carrie Finnell? She was called 'The Remote Control Girl'."

"Remote control?" Hal says. "Did she play a robot?"

"A good guess from such a clever lad," Leon tells the smirking boy. But not like he means it.

"What was her gimmick? Was she pretty?" Paul remembers he was supposed to ask that first.

"I wouldn't go calling her pretty," Leon says. "And she was too amply endowed for modern taste. But Lord in Heaven the things she could do with it all. Simply unbelievable." He seems overwhelmed by the recollection. He shakes his round, bald head, smacks his lips in a way that makes him resemble a hungry, shriveled baby.

"Did she have trained birds too?" Paul says.

"Much better than that. She had trained breasts! They could move every which way on command. And tassels. She had magical tassels."

"There ain't no such things," Hal says.

"When Carrie had them on they were. Now Picture, if you will, a voluptuous blonde. She's standing at attention center stage. There's a devilish smile on her dimpled face. A tight bodice covers her hourglass torso. Both bra cups have a long, shimmering tassel attached." He holds a gnarled finger before each half of his chest to simulate the ornament. "All of a sudden, her left breast starts popping up and down. Going zigzag. The tassel begins to twirl. Slowly at first. Then it goes faster. Faster still. Like an airplane propeller readying for flight."

His knobby finger spins as best it can. His head goes round and round, following the action with comic exaggeration. "Meanwhile the other tassel's a limp noodle. It doesn't budge an inch. Dead as a doornail. That's how much control she has. And the jerks—I mean the audience—they go wild. But she's only getting started. Soon she has the other tassel going top speed."

Leon's mangled finger revs up. He starts prancing around his make-believe stage, trilling a jazzy drum beat with his tongue. His blissful expression recalls the image of a saint in rapture. At least to Paul. He can't help wondering which the old man enjoys most, imitating the stripper or imagining himself watching her from the wings.

"But that's not all," Leon says. "Carrie has tassels on her derriere as well. She spins them like blazes while she works the other two." He shuffles across the floor. His hands shift from his chest to his bottom as he tries to reproduce the quartet of twirling fringe. His once rapturous face turns manic.

No longer entranced, Paul finds the spectacle embarrassing to watch. He doesn't need to look at his buddy to know Hal's doing a slow burn. He can feel the heat, the anger. It comes as a major relief when Leon's breathing grows labored and he sinks onto the bench under the windows, his chest heaving. His bulging eyes glaze to their palest blue. "Damn if I couldn't use a drink." His voice is a mere whisper.

"I'll get a soda from the gas station," Paul tells him.

"That's not the kind he wants," Hal says. "Is it old man?"

"Such a wonder," Leon says between puffs. "The boy's a veritable mind reader."

Paul regards the empty bottles he removed from Leon's fingers. "We can't go into bars."

"Ah, but I can. Providing I have the scratch. There's a lovely establishment right across Broadway."

Hal jumps off the bench and makes a beeline for Leon. "How'd you like to earn some money? Enough for all the rotgut you can chug in one night?"

"And who'll stand me the cash I'd like to know?"

Hal pulls a ten-spot from his pocket.

"Now that's a real surprise," Paul says.

"Some money my dad gave me."

"Only some?"

Leon examines the wrinkled bill as if it were a long sought treasure map. "What's the catch?"

"Put on a show," Hal says, "like you did for us. Only in a different place."

"Where?" Leon's eyes stay glued to the money.

Hal helps the old man to his feet.

"I'll tell you while we wait for the bus."

CHAPTER 5

THE TRIO SEPARATES in the fairly crowded bus. Hal directs Leon to a window seat and slides in next to him. Paul lands in the following row. Beside him dozes a middle-aged woman with brassy hair. Three warts of varying color garnish her ample right cheek. If he connected them with a pencil line, the growths would form a perfect triangle.

A rare trip downtown usually fills him with anticipation. The crowds, the department stores and stately office buildings, evoke a fantasy of permanent escape. But this trip causes only numb anxiety.

He tries to focus on the passing scenery. Like his former self Broadway could use a good scrub and a new wardrobe. Tired clapboard homes, some with desperate storefronts, give way to grungy apartment buildings; more lifeless sidewalks his father says once bustled with people. Eventually the bus stops at a wider intersection. Several more passengers board. They're from the huge public housing project located down a steep hill off busy McCarter Highway. The project's rooftop lights pulse red against the darkening sky. Many of the kids who live in the complex attend Paul's school, where a fragile peace among white, black and brown always threatens to implode over minor issues. Something about the massive development rouses Leon from his torpor. He nudges Hal, taps an arthritic finger on the greasy window. "There's more progress for you. Get your throat slit for a nickel down there, you will."

"Put a lid on it now." Hal glances backwards at Paul, who makes a show of taking his jacket off so he can stand, check the bus for any newly arrived faces within hearing distance of the old man. He's relieved not to see any. And he's grateful for the worn engine muffler. It makes the rumbling bus sound like a giant beehive.

Christmas decorations festoon downtown although it's only the first weekend after Thanksgiving. Red and green lights traverse the major shopping streets in high, tinseled arches secured to parallel lampposts. All the stores have elaborate holiday window displays. Bamberger's and Hahne's—the two quality establishments—easily win any competition that might exist among the many retailers, large or small. Deep in their own thoughts the boys walk half a block before realizing they've lost Leon again. They find him gazing at a gloomy parking lot packed with cars.

"What's he staring at?" Hal says. "And why can't he keep up?"

"Give him a break," Paul says. "He's old and hung over. It'd sure help if you could decide where to settle. For a guy who's always bragging about how cool he is, you sure seem nervous."

"I'm only playing it smart, scouting for the easiest mark."

"Then make up your mind. Leon's not the only one getting tired and cold." The light jacket Hal told Paul to wear doesn't offer much warmth against the chilly breeze. His shoulders are sore from scrunching them against his neck. He can't afford to get sick again. If he misses another week of school, his grades'll tank for sure. Then he'll have to deal with his parents, who'll otherwise ignore his education until the next report-card day.

"Bookend the old coot," Hal tells him as they grow near. "We'll glue him between us." To Leon he jokes, "You're in no condition to drive, hotshot." He pats the old man's back, has to rescue him from tipping forward.

"I used to work here," Leon's voice is angry. His bulging eyes, wet. His swollen hands clench tight as the knobby joints allow.

"Yeah sure," Hal says. "I can see you parking cars and handling dough."

"This ugly nothing. This tar pit filled with metal and rubber used to be the Empire Theatre. Built like a mosque, it was, and twice as beautiful. Mosaics on the walls. Paintings of exotic lands. Gorgeous women. It had a thousand seats inside. The longest balcony I ever did see. Every week we had a new show blow in from the Hirst circuit. The hottest burlesque in the country. A dozen years I worked at the Empire. Before it got raided a second time,

73

along with the Minsky Adams. Both theaters closed for good after that. Back in '57, I think. A dozen years! And what'd they give me? A lousy, one-week severance."

"What'd you do at the Empire?" Paul says.

"In the end I played the candy pitchman."

"What kind of act was it?"

"Tell us while we walk." Hal grabs the old man's arm and makes tracks. Paul falls in line.

"The candy pitchman wasn't an act, per se. It was more like theatrical retail."

"I don't get you," Hal says.

"I think he means he sold candy," Paul says.

"Got it in one," Leon shouts. "But I did give my spiel right on stage during every intermission. The lights blazed on me alone. And I worked my pitch hard. Electrifying I was. Brought in plenty of dough too. Enough to tide the place over during hard times. When I was done with my shtick, a bunch of kids flooded the aisles, delivering candy to the takers." Leon shakes his hands in the air as if signaling for help. "I used to say, 'A prize in every box!' while I waved twenty-dollar bills or a wristwatch in my paws. Something to lure the jerks into thinking they might win big."

"And did they?" Paul asks.

Leon shrugs. "Can't remember now." His tone rings false.

"That sounds like you and Hal," Paul says.

"Me and who?"

"Back at the train station. When my buddy showed you some money, and gave you *his* pitch?"

"Ah, the money. Our agreement!" Leon's sagging face turns rapturous.

"Shut the fuck up," Hal says. But he isn't talking to the old man.

At first it all happens as planned.

In the boy's section of Klein's Department Store, over a circular clothes rack, Paul watches Leon start his performance in the men's section one wide aisle away. The old man has attracted a crowd, as Hal said would happen. The shoppers are in good spirits. Some kids egg the geezer on, applaud his every move while passing sly looks. Meanwhile their parents register a mix of surprise and sorrow. Even the salesmen watch, seemingly amused by the novelty. Or reluctant to interrupt a crowd pleaser. At least for a while. Then one of them—the only guy with a rose pinned to his lapel—peels off, makes a phone call at the accessories counter. His hound-dog face looks red as the flower he wears.

With all his dramatic gesturing, Leon must be telling lame jokes in rapid succession. His fluty voice doesn't carry far enough to hear over the holiday music on the sound system. He grabs a Santa's hat from a chintzy display, tosses it on the floor. A festive beggar's bowl. He mimes taking money from an oversized wallet, tossing bill after bill into the cap as he does his routine. Paul bets he must've made a great pitchman in his day. Several women open their purses. A little boy in a coonskin cap drops in some coins with his father's approval.

"Look at the old fool go," Hal says from behind.

"Damn," Paul says, "you scared me. Where'd you disappear to?"

"Thought I'd get greedy before Leon got going. Copped me a nice sweater."

"I don't see—"

Hal lifts his own jersey a little to show the stolen one beneath. "An old trick," he says. "You go in the dressing room with a bunch of stuff, and come out wearing one under your own clothes. Piece a cake."

Paul's never seen his buddy half so happy, pleased with himself, no matter what they've done together. And all for stealing a dumb sweater. He has to turn away. No time to let hurt feelings sap his concentration.

Back in the other section, two burly men with stern faces make their way through Leon's audience. They interrupt the second act of his show.

"There's security," Hal says. "Let's get what we really came for while that mummy keeps them busy."

Paul slips a black leather coat over his thin jacket. It smells like new shoes up close, has a velvet squeak to it when he bends the fabric. Hal grabs the brown, suede number he checked out earlier. The one with wooden buttons and extra pockets inside. It's a deluxe item the discount store usually doesn't carry. They slide the empty hangers into other jackets on the circular rack. "I'll scope this area," Hal says. "You watch the creeps grilling our decoy."

"You sure they'll just kick him out like you said?"

"What else they going to do? It's almost Christmas, and the old bird's practically dead." Paul watches Leon continue to distract the security guards with his patter, his toothless smile. But they must've heard enough. They grab him by the arms, lift him slightly so he has to walk on tiptoe. "They're taking him to the elevators," he reports. "Some little kid's running after them. He's stopped them. He's got a Santa's cap in his hand. The one Leon set on the floor to beg with. Isn't that nice?"

"Real sweet," Hal says. "Keep looking."

Paul watches the guards confer over the old man's shiny head. Finally they let him take his meager earnings from the hat. Leon offers the boy his hand to shake. The little kid probably squeezes too hard. Leon lets out a howl, the only sound from him that's reached Paul's ears. "Oh boy. Everyone on the floor's staring at him."

"It's all clear our end," Hal says. "Start hauling ass."

He makes a beeline for the central escalators far from the commotion. Not once does he check to see if his buddy follows, a thing that upsets Paul, makes him feel expendable. He turns back to Leon, catches a glimpse of the man's shrunken form as the elevator closes with scary finality.

Seconds go by. But it's like he's been alone from the start. For the first time since he entered the store, he allows himself to think that he'll be the only one responsible for his actions. The only one to pay the consequences. An obvious truth always known. But one he can't repress in his seductive buddy's absence. The new coat he wears suddenly radiates unbearable heat. Its leathery smell nauseates. The fabric tightens around him like a giant black snake come to life. It's suffocating him. He peels it off and throws it on top of the rack. He trails after his pal, gone from sight. It shouldn't matter if he leaves empty handed. Not to Hal, who got what he wanted.

The escalator ride seems endless. Thank goodness it's only one level. Paul'd walk down if there weren't people in his way. None of them Hal. He stares at the grilled metal step on which he stands. It gradually loses height, glides into the toothy, flat mouth that swallows it whole. In his distraction he doesn't alight fast enough. He trips. The husky man ahead of him turns around and breaks the fall. It's almost as if the guy were waiting for him.

"Thanks mister." He doesn't look up, eager to saunter out the back exit and meet up with his buddy and Leon as planned.

But the man doesn't let go.

"What're you doing?" Paul looks at the wide, black face and knows already.

The smiling man doesn't answer. He marches the compliant boy past gawking shoppers and shiny decorations, through a discreet door tantalizingly close to an exit. Down a long hallway Paul sees his buddy getting hit by a lanky, hawk-faced man with blond hair spiked like a rooster's comb. The guy turns in Paul's direction. A chilling look of pleasure distorts his features.

The gray tiny room Paul sits in faces a huge stock area crammed with holiday goods. He answers the questions without hesitation. Home address. Phone number. Age. What could be simpler? A confession of sorts, but not to any crime. He's relieved to talk. It helps him breathe, reduces the ache in his chest. The security guy resembles a pudgy, giant frog. But he has a soothing voice. It seems to well from his ample paunch. And there's that steady smile, pleasant enough, apart from the large incisors.

"I didn't take anything," Paul tells him, not that he's been asked. "Go ahead and frisk me."

"If I wanted to I would've. But I didn't see the need, did I?"

The guard taps his fingers against the scarred wooden desk, which takes up most of the stifling room. "In this store us security are like Santa Claus. We know when you been naughty. We know when you been nice. I saw your every move out there on the floor. Not going to say how. I know you didn't steal. But your friend next door, he's a different character. Got expensive taste too. You were with him when he lifted that boss jacket. Maybe he had you play lookout while that old fool across the way panhandled. Thought he'd take advantage of the situation." The guard leans back, nibbles on a fingernail. "Now I'd call that probable cause."

"I don't know what you're talking about," Paul says.

The guard rolls his eyes. The left one has a large sty that makes the boy wince. He won't talk about Hal with this man or anyone else. Not even the cops, whom the guard called first thing. That goes for squealing on Leon as well. But the old guy must've gotten away after all, like Hal promised. That can only mean security didn't make the connection. Some Santa Clauses they are. Despite his own calamity he imagines Leon freezing on their meeting corner, waiting for his payoff, or staring angrily at that parking lot, wishing he were a pitchman again. At least he walked away with enough money to get loaded. Maybe he's blotto already.

"What happens now?" Paul knows from the guard's phone call it will involve the cops. Only minutes have passed since he got nabbed. It seems more like hours.

Before the guard can answer, there's a commotion in the room next door. A big argument. One between Hal and the frightening guard who detains him. Paul can't make out the muffled words. They have an urgent tone that escalates by the second.

"What's that guy doing to my friend?"

The guard shrugs his beefy shoulders. "I don't know. I'm not in there, am I?"

Paul stares hard at his captor, who won't return his gaze. "I need to see Hal." He stands up. The guard doesn't move a muscle. Paul can see why. No way in that cramped space can he get past the massive guy, whose swivel chair leans full against the door.

"You just worry about yourself." The guard gestures for him to sit. "Be glad you're not next door."

"Why's that?" Paul sinks back into his chair. Like never before he wishes he were strong enough to best this guard and escape with his buddy.

In the other room Hal's voice grows louder. There's a dull, thumping noise. And another. And— He hears a guttural moan. Only this time it's not Hal.

The guard cocks his head towards the other room, his face slowly registering concern.

"You better go see about my friend," Paul says like it's an order. "He's only a kid, and you'll be responsible too if . . ." His eyes well up. "My father knows a lot of cops. They all grew up together. They'd do anything for each other. My father said so. He says that about all his friends."

Resentment flashes in the guard's eyes, his smile disappears, replaced by a sneer. For a moment Paul's afraid for himself. The guard stretches his long arm, raps his fist hard against the wall. It makes a hollow sound. "Hey Alex," he says in a voice that hurts Paul's ears, "everything okay in there?" His query gets no response. He tries again, even louder, but to no avail. He grabs his phone, slams it down when there's no pick up. "I'm getting tired of that guy's shit."

"What shit?" Paul says.

"I'm locking you in." The guard jumps to his feet. His thick fingers search for the right key among the many squeezed onto a ring he unclips from his belt loop.

"Let me go with you," Paul says. "I need to see Hal's okay."

The guard ignores his plea.

"If you don't take me, I swear I'll hurt myself bad and say you did it. Then you'll have two kids to explain about."

His arm aches under the guard's tight grip as he's dragged out the room. His thigh slams against the desk corner, but he doesn't complain for fear of halting their progress.

The door to the other office opens only part way when the security guard tries to enter. He leans his fuzzy head in. "Jesus Christ, Alex!" He squeezes into the room, taking Paul with him. He forces the boy to kneel in a corner while he examines the other guard, this Alex creep, who looks much smaller crumpled on the cement and moaning. A large marble paperweight of the Statue of Liberty lies next to him. Its sharp-edged base is smeared with blood.

And there's no sign of Hal.

CHAPTER 6

THE HOLDING CELL Paul sits in at the station makes the security guard's office seem huge by comparison. He barely can move. His cell, and several empty ones like it, line a wall of the unheated garage. Even his seat is metal. Different fuel odors, all equally nauseating, fill his lungs. Chilly air blows in whenever a patrol car enters. Arriving policemen stop and peer into his cage as if he were an exotic zoo animal. One duo parks near his cell. They have someone in the back seat.

"Get your fucking hands off me," the man yells as he's dragged out.

"Not in front of the kid," a cop says.

The drunken man nails his rheumy eyes on Paul. His laughter sounds like a donkey braying.

Paul watches the trio make their way into the station, where it's warm and the air, breathable. He was in there for all of ten minutes. But then he was put outside. Why he can't figure.

One thing he does know. They don't have his buddy. Not yet. Back at the store he learned from one of the officers who collected him that Hal escaped. "Still at large," the man said into a crackling walky-talky. Paul searched for a trail of blood as he was escorted from the security guard's office. It hurts to think Hal might be injured. He tries to make his mind go blank.

A man with wavy, jet-black hair appears at the station's back entrance. Tall and lean, his approach is casual, his suit, snugly tailored. He offers the same critical grimace the other cops displayed. But his lushly framed eyes tell another story. Their calm grayness seems full of sympathy. Or maybe Paul's imagining because he's so anxious and the man, so beautiful. Like many heroes in ancient mythology. Like the Chinese prince he once thought himself to be. He wants to believe that beauty and goodness go together, although his knowing Hal has shown him otherwise.

"I'm Detective Gianetti." The man's lopsided smile dimples one cheek. His key slips into the lock. It sounds like coins falling through a candy machine. "Come with me, son." He doesn't grab as the security guard had done, but rests his hand lightly on Paul's shoulder, as if putting the boy on his honor, trusting him to acquiesce, which he does, not noticing the sticky concrete as he walks. Not feeling or thinking anything in particular, until he enters the detective's office, and sees Max sitting near a desk much like the security guard's. Then it seems a major explosion occurs in his brain. His ears ache. His jaw clamps shut. A translucent blue curtain veils his eyes. The pain in his chest feels like the time he swallowed grapes whole because he didn't want to spoil their oval perfection.

Max doesn't say a word but his mouth works plenty. He must have a pack of gum stuffed in there. His teeth chomp on the rubbery confection the way a baseball player chews tobacco. In the overheated room, his jacket exudes the odor of stale cigarette smoke. The smell reminds Paul of his mother, nowhere in sight. He's led to a seat on the opposite side of the desk. It's not nearly far enough for his liking.

"Your father and I had a talk about you." The detective looks at Max then at Paul again. "Me and your dad, we grew up together. We went into the Army together. I want to keep you out of trouble—if I can. It's all up to you, Paul. Right now you're in protective custody. Do you know what that means?"

"That you're going to protect me?"

The detective smiles, than squeezes his lips tight. "That's right. It means I'm going to find out what's best for you. Act in your best interest. It also means you're not under arrest. This is an interview, not an interrogation. Do you know the difference?"

Paul nods yes, then shakes his head.

"An interview is more informal. Less official. It's me wanting to get some facts from you. An interrogation. Now that's more serious. It means I've had a problem with what you've been saying. That I'm concerned you might've done something wrong and aren't telling me everything about it. Or aren't sorry for it. Not enough."

"I'm plenty sorry already. But not for stealing anything because I didn't."

"Since you're so young, I have a lot of choice in how to dispose your case."

"Does that mean you're going to throw it out?"

"It means," the detective says, "I can decide what'll happen to you after I've heard everything you have to say. But you have to answer all my questions truthfully. Do you understand how important that is?"

Paul nods, avoiding his father's steady gaze that heats his face. He's surprised by Max's silence. How long has he been at the station? What did the two men speak about? Their conversation seems to linger in the air, connecting them in a way that reminds Paul of Hal and himself. If only he could recapture the adults' words. Put himself in the frame beforehand. And what about the security guard who detained him? What else did that guy report?

"I didn't steal anything," he repeats. "Not a single thing. I shouldn't be here even. It isn't fair." He tries not to sound whiny since it ticks off Max, who looks like he can't endure one more tick.

"What about your friend?" the detective asks.

"What about him?"

"You watch your mouth," Max warns.

The detective gestures for him to stop.

"I wasn't being smart," Paul says. "I want to know how he is. He could be hurt somewhere. Bleeding and stuff.

Scared to come out of hiding because he might get worse. You should've seen how that guard was roughing up Hal. The creep could've broken a bone or something."

"Quit that crying," his father orders.

Which only turns on the faucets more.

"Max," the detective says, "you're only here as an observer. I'll have to do this alone if you can't—"

"Okay, okay," Max tells him.

"I doubt your friend's hurt," the detective says. "He managed to knock the guard nearly unconscious. And he slipped out the store without drawing any attention."

"Only to protect himself." Paul remembers seeing blood on the heavy-looking paperweight next to the prone man, not knowing for sure whose blood it might be. "Hal kept yelling for the guy to stop hitting him. I know for a fact. I was next door with that fat black guard, who kept smiling while Hal got slapped." He leans over the desk, studies his questioner. "Do the police let security guards beat up kids for fun? I saw that man's face when he and Hal were in the hallway. He looked right at me. That guy was enjoying himself."

Paul can see he's hit a nerve, come upon a weakness. Max and the detective regard each other with unease. Surely they must think the guard's actions are much worse than a simple theft. Why aren't there questions about Hal's treatment? On his ride to the station, Paul kept telling the cops who picked him up all about the assault. They kept ignoring him. How he wishes now he'd spent his time in that tiny cell reviewing his story. Polishing it to a high gloss as if it were one of his shop projects.

"I warned him months ago not to hang out with that kid," Max says.

"And I didn't," Paul says. "Ever since you told me not to. Ask Mom if she saw me with him. Or if he ever came up to the apartment again. I went downtown all by myself. Ran into Hal there. We walked around looking at the Christmas decorations like a lot of kids were doing. Eventually we wound up at Klein's."

"Where your friend stole an expensive jacket while you were with him," the detective says.

"I didn't *see* him steal anything. Honest. I was busy looking at some old bum in the men's department across the way. The guy was putting on a show for handouts. Everyone in the place watched him. He was clowning it up big-time. Ask any of the store clerks. They were looking too. After some men hauled him away, I turned back to Hal and saw he was gone. I left the boy's department with nothing that wasn't mine."

His own deceit makes him consider a chilling possibility.

"Did that security guard say I stole something? If he did, the guy's a big fat liar."

"No one's accused you of stealing," the detective says. "But I'd like to know—just between us—did you *intend* to steal, then change your mind?"

Paul shakes his head with such vigor it makes him dizzy.

"What about your friend, Hal? Did you know what he was going to do? Did you *intend* to help him, then have second thoughts?"

There's that damn word again. "He never said anything to me about wanting to steal. Not once. Not even a hint. If he had, I wouldn't've hung with him, much less help out. Why should I?"

He can't tell from the detective's impassive gaze whether his story-on-the-fly is getting traction. "You can't blame me. Not for what Hal might've done on his own. Since when am I guilty for him or what he's thinking? Like I told you, I ran into the kid downtown. I'm sorry I went now. Sorry I ever got to know him in the first place." His tears start to flow again, and for many different reasons. One being he feels like a traitor. "Something like this has never happened before."

"I know that," the detective says. "Otherwise, I'd be treating you differently, no matter what good friends me and your dad are." He takes his time filling out a form in his tidy, cramped script. He checks the boxes he's filled. The paper's upside down but Paul can read the title. Already he feels betrayed. "That says 'Juvenile Investigation Report'."

"Yes it does. That's what you are—a juvenile."

"But you told me this was only an interview. Informal like."

"And it is."

"So why do you have to make a report?" Whenever Paul gets a write-up in school, it always leads to more trouble, and a bigger file.

"The law requires me to," the detective tells him. "Anytime the police have contact with a juvenile, we have to make a record of it. I'd do the same if you were the victim of a crime, instead of—"

"But I didn't commit a crime."

"I wasn't going to say you had. But you're involved in one, if only because you were present when it happened."

"What do you mean *if* only?"

The detective makes a show of putting down his pen, signaling a truce of sorts. "Look, son. We have quite a ways to go. There's more I need to ask about the incident. Let's start from the beginning again. But first, are you thirsty? Do you need to use the bathroom?"

"Yes."

"Which one? Or both?" The detective offers a lopsided smile.

"Just water."

"Just water, what?" Max says.

"Just water, please."

Paul watches air bubbles rise up the half-full cooler. The flimsy cup is cone-shaped, awkward to pass along. The detective wraps his free hand over the boy's outstretched one to guide the transfer. Their eyes meet and hold. Paul grows breathless and blushing. He brings the paper cone to his lips, barely sipping. He repeats the gesture many times until there's nothing left to drink.

For nearly a half-hour the detective asks more questions. Most of them versions of what he'd asked before, only more subtle, with many embellishments—and the occasional lengthy detour to subjects like home life and school. In particular how Paul feels about his parents' separation. Is he angry about it? Does it make him want to do things he knows are wrong? And what about his relationship with Hal? How would he describe it? What did they do together? Did he know Hal was arrested for shoplifting before?—a revelation that makes Paul angry with his friend, while not really being surprised.

The interview reminds him of what lawyers do on TV when they want to trick a witness at trial. His brain seems on fire. And despite his anxiety he feels immensely alive. The way he did at the creek when Hal pulled his dangling body to safety. But now it's Paul himself who does the heavy lifting. He sticks to his story with a focused clarity he's never experienced before. He keeps his tale simple. Politely corrects whenever he's misquoted or the detective tries to add information he didn't supply. He's amazed at how well he can lie in front of Max and to the officer, whose friendliness, whose luminous beauty, almost tempts him, in fleeting moments of weakness, to recant, to tell the whole truth and nothing but.

A lull in the gentle examination occurs. The radiator behind him makes a dull, clanking sound; its regulator hisses like an angry cat. Another detective lumbers in, grumbling to himself. Paul watches the stocky, gray-haired man retrieve papers from some filing cabinets near a cluttered desk. The cabinets are made of wood. Their scarred framework reminds him of the card catalogue in the public library. How he wishes he were there instead, sitting in his favorite chair, lost in a book, or talking to the pretty librarian who'll be getting married in spring. Grimy waves of shame pore over him when he glances at Max.

Detective Gianetti rolls the pen in his fingers as if it were a string of rosary beads. "So, how did you like the cell you were in?" he says.

"What?" Paul's thrown by the change in topic. "You mean in the garage?"

The detective nods.

"I hated it." What else could the man think?

"Your father and me wanted to give you a taste of what prison's like. The cells there aren't much bigger, you know. They smell bad too. And you have to share them with other kids. Kids a lot tougher than you. Kids who could make your life miserable." The detective leans back in his chair and grimaces. "Yes sir. Be a shame if you ever had to live in one of those cells day in, day out."

Speechless at the idea Paul can only nod. Perhaps he's not such a good liar after all. Maybe he's made a big mistake, should've confessed about everything. Even Leon. Maybe every lie he's told shows on his face, in his eyes, clear as the form the detective writes on.

"I've decided to let you go with a caution."

"With who?" Paul says, only half-hearing.

"A caution. A serious, last-chance warning to stay out of trouble. I'm referring you to your parents' care. You can go home. But I expect you to do everything they tell you, and behave like the responsible kid I think you can be. I'm giving your mom and dad a lot of suggestions to help you along. And I'll be checking up on you every now and then." He reaches into a drawer filled with thick pamphlets, selects a dozen or so. The top one's named *Guiding the Adolescent.* He hands them to Max, whose loud sigh turns into a hacking cough that causes him to visit the water cooler.

Paul considers the stack of thick brochures. He can't imagine his father reading more than two at most. "I'm really sorry all this happened. You don't know how much I wish it were yesterday again." He wants to ask about Hal, what will happen to him. How he can help. But he can't. Not with his father glaring at him. Not after he expressed regret at ever knowing the kid, and even promised to tell if he heard from him.

"We're going to find your friend," the detective says. "And when we do, you may have to appear in court as a witness. It all depends on how our investigation goes. What charges are pressed against him by the store—and the guard he assaulted. How Hal pleas. As things look now, the boy's in a lot of trouble."

"But what about him getting beat up?"

"We'll be investigating that too. And there's always a good chance that Hal's story is different from yours. He might say you and he went to the store to shoplift together. That you chickened out. Or that stealing was all *your* idea. In that case, you and I'll need to have another kind of talk."

"That won't happen," Paul says, with as much conviction as he can muster.

The detective leans in close, gazes at his charge for what seems like a long time. He wets his full lips, opens his mouth to speak.

Paul imagines himself falling in.

CHAPTER 7

MAX'S SILENCE IN the car baffles Paul and fills him with concern. His father always yells when angry. Sometimes worse. This evening should've caused an explosion. He wonders what Max and Detective Gianetti talked about while he waited outside the office. All he could hear was his father holler about giving up.

His rumination jolts to a halt when the car bounces and swerves. The right front tire flops beneath him like a clown's giant shoe. Its hubcap rolls across the pavement. He hears the sound of metal hitting metal. The cap spins into silence.

"Frigging retread." Max swings into the driveway of Mt. Pleasant Cemetery, past the gothic-inspired gates that point at the sky. Paul imagines a ghoul appearing behind those high, rusting bars. The monster's rotting skin is lit to a spectral sheen by the car's low beams, like in a horror movie about dumb teenagers who park in secluded places.

"Find the hub cap," Max says. "It didn't go far."

He cuts the lights and the engine, lumbers to the trunk for a spare, yet another retread. He curses all the way. He's even better than Hal at stringing swear words together without repetition. Paul slowly exhales to the cussing. It could be a good sign if father and son need to take a breath together.

Max peers over the trunk door. "What'd I tell you?"

Paul jumps out his side to begin the hunt. Alert to anything untoward, he heads for the cemetery gates, gone dark and gloomy with the car's headlights off. The hubcap must've struck the gates to make that pinging noise he heard. He'd rather the cap were across Broadway near the castle, another gothic-inspired structure built a century earlier. One that features an impressive turret. Paul knows it's really a pharmacy school, but he likes to pretend otherwise. It's one of many fortress-like buildings he imagines living in with Hal. Or he did before tonight.

He spots the hubcap lying in a puddle behind a holly bush near the gates. Mindful of thorny leaves he reaches in. If only he could find his friend with the same ease, a baby Moses in the bulrushes, but with Max and the cops well out of the picture. He can't afford to worry about Hal right now, must stay on guard for the certain fallout. It could happen any time. He regards his distorted image in the hubcap. His friend smiles back. But where's the extra light coming from? He turns around. The windows of the caretaker's cottage glow yellow. A portly man with thick glasses appears at one of them. He's wearing a striped robe, its collar wrapped around his neck, up to his jug ears. The guy must've been asleep. His puff of gray hair swirls up to a point.

"What're you doing here at this time of night?" he says once he gets the reluctant window to stay open. "What's that you're holding?" He pronounces his w's like v's. His garbled speech sounds as if his mouth were full of syrup.

"Don't worry, Mister, it's only a hubcap. We got ourselves a flat." Paul gestures at the old black Chevy sedan, where his father noisily rearranges the trunk.

"You say something?" Max peers over the dented hood, sees his son's not alone. The two men regard each other and nod.

"Too bad for you," the man says. "I'm the caretaker here. I can make a call if you want."

"Thanks, but I got it under control."

The caretaker nods again, but doesn't leave the window, barred like the cell Paul was in not long ago. Maybe the guy's lonely. Who wouldn't be living in a cemetery? To say nothing of scared, especially at night. The man has a pad and pencil. He squints at the car, writes something down. Probably the license number. Does every adult in charge of anything have to make a report, even for the smallest problem?

"We had vandals a while ago," the caretaker says. "On Halloween. Jumped the back gate, they did. Wrote obscene things on some of our finest statues. Turned over a few gravestones. You maybe read about it in *The Star Ledger*? These kids of today. They got no respect for the sacred."

"The sacred what?" Paul says.

The man looks indignant. "This cemetery. Every inch of its forty acres is sanctified. Like a church. You should know that."

"I do now."

"Mt. Pleasant is Newark's high society burial place. All the best families are here. We've got the Ballantines, the Frelinghuysens, the—"

"Get over here and help," Max says, while the man finishes his list.

He instructs his son to fold a crumpled army blanket four times over. Paul drapes it on the front hood for better handling. At first the khaki woolen fabric itches, but he gets used to its roughness. Max drags the spare out and lays it on the ground. Even the chilly air can't suppress the strong odor of grease, decaying rubber and dirt. His father has a similar smell whenever he stops by the apartment after work.

"This blanket still has sand in it." Paul rubs the grit between his fingers.

"So what? We're not going to sleep in it."

"The sand must be from when we went to the beach. You and Mom and me." It was two years ago, but Paul recalls the vacation well. He was so relieved not to have any fighting or disapproval, the last day he almost swallowed all his mother's nervous pills rather than return home. Instead he took one and fell dead asleep in the car. "I had fun that week."

"Did you have fun tonight? Are you having fun now?"

Paul shakes his head solemnly.

"Well neither am I."

"Is there something wrong?" The caretaker's small plump fingers curl around the bars.

"Couldn't be better." Max takes a deep breath, regards his son with such cavernous disappointment it makes the boy want to disappear. "Try and help your old man for once."

"That's what I'm doing." Paul holds out the finished blanket as proof.

"On the ground," Max tells him.

"What?"

"Put it on the ground in front of the flat. We got to protect our knees."

"You didn't say to."

"You should've figured it out." Max looks up from the spare he's inspecting. "Call that a fold?"

"It's hard to do all alone. When Mom and me fold sheets, we do them together because they're so long."

Max grabs the blanket and starts over, assigning his son two corners. He takes the remaining pair. "In the Army, you learn to do things by yourself."

"We're not in the Army."

"Don't get wise."

"I'm only saying." If his old man wanted the blanket so neat, why wasn't it folded right when it was in the trunk?

"I might've stayed in the service after the war," Max says, "if I had it to do all over again. I'd've gotten more schooling too. Become a first-class radio specialist. Maybe take a good long time getting married." A pained expression fills his square face. His gaze seems distant.

"Mom says you could've gone to college after your discharge like Uncle Vince. Or started your own business like Uncle Bunny. She says we can still buy a house on the cheap with that Army bill. Then we could move to the suburbs."

"And live happily ever after," Max says. "That's enough."

He lays out the folded blanket as if some drill sergeant were to inspect it. For a young man he grunts a lot whenever he bends. And he has to light up a cigarette before laying into any project. The cancer stick dangles from his chapped lips like a mentholated straw. His left eye flutters against the smoke. It's hard to believe he and Detective Gianetti are the same age. Max's face has a lot more lines. And they're deeper. His body's thicker too around the stomach.

He uses a special wrench to loosen the wheel's lug bolts. It's shaped like a giant pick-up jack. The work doesn't come easily. Sometimes he presses his foot on one of the tool's arms to get the action going. "You got to be careful when you do this. Too much pressure and you could strip the fitting. Then you're screwed."

"Just like the bolt," Paul says.

"Wise guy," Max says, but with a grin. "After I loosen them all, you can finish the job."

"You want me to change the tire myself?"

"Of course not. Take out the bolts and stick them in the hubcap. I don't want them disappearing on us."

"Or then we're screwed?"

But his father's not amused this time. "Got to jack up the car first."

"Why's that?" Paul's not really interested, but he knows his father likes explaining anything mechanical.

"Because it's dangerous otherwise. The tire could get unstable and collapse. I always remove the bolt that's in the three o'clock position first. Work my way around. The top one I save for last. This way the wheel stays in place until the final piece comes out."

"I'll do it exactly like you," Paul says.

Max looks pleased. His body seems to relax. He even stubs out the half-finished cigarette. Usually he works a smoke to its filter, unless he puts it down somewhere, forgets about it, then lights another, sometimes even a third, depending on how far he paces—and if he's had a few too many beers.

"Excuse me, my friend," the caretaker says. "I swept that driveway clean earlier this evening."

Max exudes a slow grunt. He ignores the implicit request.

Paul retrieves the stub, holds it for the man to see. "I'll stick it in the ashtray." He reaches into the open passenger window, places the stub on top of many others. They form a precarious mound.

"You're a good boy," the caretaker tells him, like he's surprised.

The praise seems to steam Max more. "You're a good boy, all right. That's why we're stuck here with a flat. Because you're such a good boy."

And just when Paul thought he was making headway.

"Help me find the right contact point for the jack." Max hands his son a stained and wrinkled manual opened to the relevant page. "Look at the diagram. Tell me where you think it should go."

The illustration's packed with tiny words linked to a maze of fine lines. They all lead to the chassis figure centered on the page. Paul locates the right contact his first try. His father cranks up the car after a few wobbly attempts with the screeching jack.

"Everything going all right?" the caretaker says from his barred window.

Max sits back on his haunches and lights another cigarette. "This guy's starting to get on my nerves."

"We're doing fine, Mister," Paul says. "Halfway there."

"Take your time, then. A job worth doing is worth doing well."

"He's like a goddamn foreman," Max grumbles. "Everyone's telling me what to do tonight. How to take care of my kid. How to fix a flat."

"Maybe he doesn't have a TV."

"You call this entertainment?"

"Maybe he does. I can't see living inside a graveyard, even if it's supposed to be sacred."

"Guess you'd have to be a pretty odd duck," Max says. "Or desperate." He gives Paul a hard look. "But it's his job. And you should never slam the dignity of labor. Honest work is the only decent way to get what you want in life."

"But I didn't slam the guy's job, you did. At least at first."

"You and your mother always got to win an argument."

"I wasn't arguing."

"What do you call back-talking your old man as if nothing awful, nothing shameful, happened tonight."

"Sorry." Paul reaches for a lug bolt, starts his chore before his father can ask what's keeping him.

"Does that piece look like it's at three o'clock?" Max says.

"Oh, right. Guess I was thinking in a different time zone."

"You're a real comedian for a kid who caused a shitload of trouble."

Paul begins removing the bolts and placing them in the hubcap. He wants to show he can work with speed and skill. But the last bolt slips from his hand. It rolls under the car almost dead center.

"Son of a bitch," Max says. "What'd I say about being careful."

"Anything wrong?" the caretaker asks again.

"What is this guy, a frigging windup doll?" Max signals a dismissive okay, spreads out the blanket and lies on it as he hunts for the wayward bolt.

Paul watches half his father's torso disappear under the chassis. He imagines the jack suddenly, mysteriously, losing its grip. The car crashes down with a sickening thud. Max screams for help. He's pinned to the ground in agony. And what does his son do? He comes to the rescue with amazing presence of mind for a boy his age. Or he does nothing. Only gazes at the horrible scene without emotion. The calls for help fall silent. His father's body grows still forever. Either way, the accident's all his fault. If he hadn't dropped—"

"Got it!" With some effort, Max sidles clear of the car. He finds Paul on his knees, both hands pressed hard against the base of the jack. "What're you doing?"

"Making sure the thing didn't move. It squeaked and wobbled a lot when you hiked it up, remember?"

"That's no way to keep . . ." Max squeezes his lips hard. "You did good. Looking out for your old man without being asked." He grabs his son and hugs him. Paul's nose flattens against the rough flannel shirt. He breathes through his mouth. Sideways at least. Dry cold air makes his throat ticklish. But he doesn't complain. He's not sure, but he thinks he likes getting bear-hugged. Can't remember when he had one last. If only he and Max could end the night this way.

"Is everything all right," the caretaker calls out. "Did the boy get hurt?"

"Jesus Christ, already." Max screws up his face, mimics the man to perfection.

"What're you two laughing at?" the caretaker asks. "You think maybe I'm a funny person?" He makes another note on his pad. "I'm responsible for what happens on this property. I could insist that you leave immediately."

"We weren't laughing at you, Mister," Paul says. "Honest. I cracked a joke is all."

"A joke? What kind of joke?"

"A *private* one," Max says, like the subject's closed. He refolds the blanket by himself, arranges it beside the tire. He grabs the flat so hard it sounds like a double slap. With a few deft moves, he pulls the tire straight toward him and off its mounting. "Roll it behind the trunk and lay it on the ground. We'll pack it up later."

Paul spins the tire with ease. He lets it drop to its side, causing a hard, plopping noise.

"Watch out for the macadam," the caretaker says.

"Mac who?" Paul looks around.

"She's talking about the driveway," Max says. "The black stuff's called macadam."

"Why'd you call him 'she'?"

"Because he bitches like an old lady."

Paul keeps his head down. He hopes the caretaker didn't hear. The guy might make them leave before they're finished. "What's next?"

"What do you think?"

Maybe there's some obscure step that's left before doing the obvious, but Paul can't think of one. "We put on the tire?"

"You had me worried there."

"About what?"

"I expect to see a better report card this time around."

Where'd that come from? "You will," Paul says. Though he won't say how much better. Not tonight.

Max grabs the spare tire, lines it up with the holes encircling the axle. "Take one side and hold it steady. We'll do this thing together. All you got to do is slide the rim in until it hugs the axle."

Even half the tire feels heavy when Paul helps lift it. The metal rim chimes as it settles into the cupped mounting surface.

"Put the bolts back in," Max says. "And don't drop any this time."

"I won't."

"I'll hand them to you to make sure." Max kneels beside his son. He reaches for the hubcap that holds the five bolts.

"That's the wrong way," Paul says when he's offered the end instead of the head.

106

"I was testing you."

"Yeah, I bet." Paul can't believe how well he's getting along with his old man. He's sure it has something to do with Detective Gianetti. That private talk. He probably should ask about it now, out in the open, with that nosy caretaker looking on. People often behave better when they're being watched by strangers. At least kids do. Then he might get a better idea what to expect at home.

"What'd you and your friend talk about?" He tries to sound casual.

"I got lots of friends."

"I mean your detective friend. After he told me to wait outside."

"Giancarlo."

"No, Gianetti."

"His first name's Giancarlo. We called him G.G. when we were boys."

"I didn't know."

"There's a lot you don't know, you kids today."

"Now you sound like the caretaker."

"Don't get wise. I'm being serious here, understand?"

"Loud and clear." Paul waits for more. He slows his work with the bolts to assure he won't lose concentration while he listens. And it seems more respectful somehow. "So what'd you talk about?"

"You got no idea what it's like growing up poor," Max says. "I mean Great Depression poor. The years before your grandfather got steady relief work. He was out of a job a long time. All those mouths to feed and always flat broke. That was when your Uncle Sonny took off on his own. Twelve years old! Didn't want to be a burden. Never did come back. And I know he would've if he was still alive." His long sigh turns into a hacking cough. He takes a drag of his cigarette, hands his son another bolt.

"For a long time us kids got nothing for dinner but a slice of stale bread dipped in olive oil. Maybe a teaspoon of grated cheese on top. Some vegetables from our tiny section of the yard. If they were in season. And if some prick didn't hop the fence and swipe them late at night. We owed the landlord, the grocers, the electric…"

Paul listens with the same expression he uses at funerals when he's supposed to be sad but really isn't. He's heard the story since forever and at the slightest provocation. With each recap he hates it a little more. Hates his father for telling it only to make him feel grateful for being miserable. As if a kid was a dog. Give him enough food and a place to sleep and he's good. The Depression's long over anyway. Why keep living as if it weren't? As if you prefer it to now? He's sorry he ever asked about the detective, not that his question ever got answered. He looks down at the jack. For a moment he wishes it had slipped.

"Switch places with me," Max says after his son finishes with the bolts. He leans sideways and grabs the wrench. "I'm only tightening them a little. We'll make them real snug once the tire's on the ground." He gives the first bolt a few turns, then works on the opposite one until he completes them all. With a calloused finger he draws a five-pointed star on the car's sooty black paint. "That's how you do it to keep the tire even."

"I got you," Paul says.

"How about getting the jack too?"

"You want *me* to let the car down?"

"Work it a notch at a time. It's so easy even an old lady can do it." Max thumbs back to the caretaker, who's still at the window, squinting out at the driveway with his mouth open.

Paul pretends to like his father's joke. But it reminds him of all the times Hal berated him for doing or saying something a girl'd do. At least in that way his buddy and Max have a lot in common. If only the two could meet again for the first time.

"Before my father got a steady job," Max says, slipping back into the Depression, "us kids had to do things we knew were wrong. Things we were ashamed of."

"Working this jack reminds me of pumping water," Paul tells him. "Remember how I did that on great-grand pop's farm when he was still alive?"

"Your old man's trying to teach you something important, here."

"I heard you."

"So what'd I say?"

Paul repeats his father's words almost verbatim.

"If you were a regular kid you'd find that interesting."

"I do. It's only…"

"Only what?"

"You told me all about the Depression a whole bunch of times." The look on Max's face makes him instantly regret his words. He might as well have called his father a dirty name.

"Did I ever tell you me and your uncles stole coal off the railroad cars whenever we could?" Max says. "Or swiped blocks of ice off the ice truck? Or milk and eggs from the milkman when he didn't have his brat kid riding with him?"

"I don't think so."

"You want to know why?"

Paul shrugs. "Because you were ashamed, like you said?"

"That's right. I was very ashamed. So ashamed us boys never talked about it with our parents. Not once. We showed up with whatever we could lay our hands on—if we got lucky. Didn't say a word. Mom'd cry. Pop too sometimes. They knew, of course. It was awful watching them. But us kids took from necessity. We took to survive, keep the family together. That's a lot different from what your friend did tonight. Stealing only because he wanted to. Because he's a greedy little good-for-nothing punk."

With the tire firmly on the ground, Paul slides the jack

away from the car. Exhaustion, hunger and thirst overtake him like a heavy gray wave. He hopes Max will let him have some dinner, won't insist he stay up all night in the brightly lit kitchen thinking about what happened. He's pretty sure nothing worse is on the agenda. Not from the way Max's been acting. He grabs the wrench. "Should I tighten up the bolts now?"

"I'll do it." Max works in methodical silence until he reaches the final piece in the star pattern. "Keeping your family together's important. It's everything. A man can lose himself if he loses his family. A boy needs a mother and a father to grow up right, especially when one of them can get a little crazy."

Paul doesn't have to ask which parent Max means, though he thinks the description could apply to them both. Their son twice as much, until recently. Until Hal. He can't help thinking what life was like before his buddy. What life might be without him. Stinky Paulie again. Maybe worse.

"What I'm trying to tell you," Max says, "is that I should come back home again to live. Tonight only proves it."

"Proves what?"

"That you need your old man around regular. Like I've been telling your mom a long time." Max finishes the final bolt. Has another go-round with the other pieces to assure their tightness. "Giancarlo'll give her a call tomorrow. Maybe come and talk with her."

"But I don't get it," Paul says. "When you did live with

111

us you weren't home much at all. That's why you and Mom broke up, right? She said so herself." She said a lot of other things as well about her in-laws. And the guys in the club. But he wouldn't dare repeat them. He remembers the frequent fights when Max lived at home. Utensils and plates flying in the air. His father turning over the kitchen table, storming out the apartment and down to the club. Not returning until late—and drunk.

"Things'll be a lot different this time." Max wraps his arm around his son's shoulder. "You want your old man home again, don't you?" He squeezes tighter, almost like a headlock.

"Sure I do." Paul can't get himself to meet his father's gaze. His shoulders stiffen.

"Sure you do," Max says. "Now get me the hubcap." He hums one of his favorite Big Band tunes while he refits the cap. Father and son load the flat, the tools and blanket into the trunk.

"Make sure you don't forget anything," the caretaker says, still at his window. He makes another note.

"Oh we won't." Max offers a friendly wave. He backs up the car, turns the wheels sharply so the passenger's side faces the cottage. "Give me that ashtray. And don't spill any."

Paul's careful to do it right.

Max dumps the mound of cigarette butts out his window as the car crawls down the driveway and onto the street.

CHAPTER 8

"YOU'VE GOT SOME bare spots here and here," Lenora says. "And all along that area." She reclines on her parlor couch, waving her cigarette in a zigzag motion.

Paul has trouble following her gesture. He steps away from the Christmas tree for a better view. "What do we have left?"

"Let me check." With her foot Lenora nudges an empty box lying on the floor. It collides with a stack of others Paul assembled as he worked, tipping them over. She scans the boxes for ornaments he might've missed. "Nope. Only tinsel." She seems a little drunk, even though she doesn't indulge, except for the occasional daiquiri. Must be her new pills. The nighttime ones. They have the opposite effect of the pink tablets, new as well, that energize her days.

Paul takes some long silver strands meant to represent icicles. He shimmies them close to his ear. They sound like dry grass in a breeze, remind him of the hula skirt a girl wore at his school's Halloween show. He drapes the shiny tinsel on a branch. The chubby Norwegian spruce rises over six feet. It's a tree like many others sold at the parish church he's secretly vowed never to attend again.

His father bought the fragrant evergreen a few days ago.

It was a surprise. Max is full of surprises lately. Ever since his son's brush with the law. He even took Lenora out to a movie twice in one week! It's been a long time since Paul's parents went anywhere together that wasn't a family obligation. The kind his mother hates. There was a bowling league affair two years ago. But that night ended badly. Max got drunk and had to crawl upstairs to the flat. Then he collapsed on the couch singing "Sentimental Journey" before he conked out.

Lenora's attention shifts from the tree to the holiday drama on TV. One sponsored by a greeting card company. "You know what? I think she's going to take him back." Her words emerge in a smoke cloud.

Paul looks at the handsome, estranged couple on screen. "You think so or know so?"

"I've never seen this program before. It's a worldwide premiere."

"But it's still a Christmas story. The guy's been nice to her since before the first commercial, even when she's been a royal pain. And he keeps saying he's changed. That their kid needs a father."

"Talk is cheap," Lenora says, like she's enjoying a private joke.

"How about that gift he gave her she always wanted? That wasn't cheap."

She seems to mull over the question. "It wouldn't surprise me if he bought it secondhand. Where's the receipt?"

"It was a present."

"But she might have to take it back if she doesn't want to reconcile."

"I doubt she'd return the gift, along with all the others."

"Why not?"

"I don't think she's the type."

"The type?" Lenora's face stiffens. She wraps her new kimono-style robe tighter around her chest. Some dancing white cranes disappear in the folds. "So Mr. Shakespeare, how do you think the story'll end?"

Paul shrugs.

"No, I really want to know." With some effort she sits up, looks at her son intently. "How'd you like the story to finish if you could write the ending?"

"I don't care one way or the other. It's only a movie, right?"

"Right," she says after a long pause. She taps her toes on the floor in search of her slippers, which somehow migrated under the aqua-colored couch. "Since you don't care how the story ends, I'll watch the rest in my room. Unless you need more help with the tree."

Paul looks at the mess of boxes she made on the floor. "No thanks, I'll be fine."

Lenora stops midway and snaps her fingers. "I just remembered. We got more ornaments stashed in one of your bedroom closets. They're on a back shelf somewhere."

"I'll go find them." He rummages in his closets until he

115

finds the cache of hand-painted glass ornaments. In the parlor he turns off the broadcast once Lenora's door slides shut, and he can hear muffled voices from the new portable TV Max bought her. Or is it secondhand? He switches off the table lamp and turns on the tree lights. They're designed to resemble small candles complete with holders. Each tiny light bulb is enclosed in a colorful plastic base. The candle part is filled with tinted liquid; red, yellow, green or blue. When they heat up the candles bubble. They animate every branch with constant movement, making the sea-green spruce appear vaguely aquatic.

If Paul had his way the evergreen would have nothing on it but lights. He decides to finish decorating tomorrow. He sits against the wall behind the tree, buries his head near the bare branches. He crushes some needles between his fingers. They release a pure, piney aroma unsullied by cigarette smoke. He suspects that soon, probably before Christmas, the flat will have even more smoke, the mentholated kind that gives him a headache, makes him long even more for fresh air.

Later that night he dreams about the bubbling Christmas lights, the fluid purring they make up close. The relaxing sound amplifies. It turns into a steady tapping, as if the bubbles wanted to escape. Simple line faces appear on them. Frowning faces. Desperate faces that vanish once the bubbles rupture at the surface. The lights start to explode in scattershot fashion. Each candle makes a popping noise a shade louder than its predecessor. The last awakens him. Curled against his second pillow, still more in the dream than out, he worries he'll get blamed for the mess.

Worse yet, the tapping hasn't stopped. What if the lights really are bursting? What if they burn down the place? He imagines Lenora being pleased. At least then they'd have to move.

Eyes closed he listens hard, realizes the noise doesn't come from the parlor or anywhere else in the flat. It comes from outside. At his back window. Made *by* his window. Probably the storm glass rattling, although he doesn't hear the whistling that accompanies blustery weather. The tapping grows more insistent. It has a steady beat. A syncopated rhythm no wind can create. His heart races. His shoulders ache with tension. Visions of movie monsters, hairy and reptilian, flash in his mind. A hideous man wants to lure him to certain death. And what about Lenora?

Like a cat he springs off his bed. He reaches into his closet for a baseball bat he never uses for sport. He holds his breath, peeks through the gauzy blue curtains. The venetian blind, shut tight, offers no hint of what's outside, lying in wait on the back roof of the men's club. Not even a few telling slivers appear between the dusty slats. He grabs the frayed drawstring, tugs lightly. Nothing happens. He pulls harder. Harder still. The blind at last obeys. He sees a form in the darkness and jumps back. He hears a voice,

117

subdued but unmistakable. He raises the blind, half wondering if he's still asleep.

Hal's really out there, bent low on the tar paper. His large hands are cupped around his mouth, pressed against the window pane, tunneling words through the glass, frosted with his breath.

"Open up. It's fucking cold out here."

Paul works fast. Hal seems unsteady, a dangerous thing since he's near the roof's side edge. Free to enter he tumbles over the night table. He lands on his back with a thump. Paul kneels beside the laughing boy, gestures for silence. He opens his door, listens for any sound of his mother stirring, ready to say he tripped on his way back from the john. Once certain it's safe he shuts the door.

"You okay?"

"Couldn't be better."

"Couldn't be...what're you doing here?"

Hal frowns. His eyes narrow. "I can split if you like. Don't want to spoil your frigging beauty sleep."

"You're not going anywhere. I'm worried is all. About you. The crazy way you came in." Paul thumbs at the window, still open. He goes to shut it. The air's chilly already since the heat stays low at night. He turns around, finds his buddy standing close behind.

"Boo!" Hal laughs. "Still a scaredy-cat, I see."

"You have to calm down or we'll get caught. I can't lock the door anymore. My mom took the key." Paul opens the blind of his other window. In scant light he examines his buddy's face, searches for any lingering wound from the store guard's assault.

Hal slips off his coat and throws it on the bed. "Look familiar?"

"It's the coat you wanted to swipe."

"Did swipe. Walked out the store like any other shopper." Hal makes a fist and smacks it against his open hand. "That motherless mother-fucker. I creamed him so good. Used the paperweight on him like a sledge hammer soon as he let his eyes off me."

"I was real worried you were hurt but afraid to get help."

"I got help all right." Hal doesn't sound happy about it.

"Then you were hurt."

"Just got my face smacked raw. It ain't like that prick used his fists or busted my bones."

"Sure sounded that way from the room I got put in."

"And look who walked out." Hal spreads his arms in victory. In only a few weeks he seems taller, his voice, a little deeper. But he's still wobbly from his tumble.

"You better sit down. That was a rough somersault."

Hal plops onto the double bed as if it were a trampoline and stretches his limbs. His feet dangle from the mattress. He slips off one shoe then the other. Paul catches both as they fall to keep them from making noise. One of the soles has a small hole. If he didn't know better, he'd think his buddy wanted more trouble, might even want to get caught.

"What's wrong?"

"You got to ask?"

"I mean right now. The way you're acting."

"How'm I acting?"

"Like you don't care."

"About what?"

"What happens to you."

"I know what'll happen to me. Got it all figured out."

"For real?"

"No, for fake. You're the dreamer."

"Maybe, but I'm not on the lam." Paul kneels on the bed next to his secret visitor. He has so many questions to ask, doesn't know where to start without ticking off his buddy, whose mood he finds impossible to gauge. He makes a cautious start. "You thirsty or hungry? I'll try and get anything you want." More than ever he's glad Lenora's stocking the kitchen better.

"I'm good. Stuffed myself at the party."

"The party?" In his worst imaginings, on which he often dwelled, Paul saw his buddy in an alleyway living off scraps.

"Way up in Belleville," Hal says, "But I got out at the tracks."

"Out of what?"

"The car."

"There was a party in a car?"

"Of course not. I told you it was in Belleville. A *house*

in Belleville. Classy. Lots of nice rooms. I was riding back when it was over. Decided to pay you a visit."

"Was someone driving you home?" Paul waits and waits, but his buddy doesn't answer, only stares at the sloped ceiling. "So where've you been the past two weeks? When you didn't show at school, or anywhere else I could think of, I called your place to see if you were there. Or in jail maybe. Your mom got all hysterical. She yelled that she didn't know where you were. Told me never to call again. Then she slammed the phone down." Since his buddy always insisted on calling him, it was the first time Paul ever heard the woman's voice. After that he was glad he got cold feet and hadn't tried to see her.

Hal lets out a long sigh that smells of alcohol. "My mom wasn't angry at you. She was worried about the cops. They might have the phone tapped or something. Might have the neighborhood patrol car doing special watch on the place. That's how my brother Richie got snatched. And what're you griping about? Here you are sacked out in your own bed. It ain't like you're in trouble. Shit, you didn't steal nothing, much less whack a guard flat with a paperweight. The cops can't touch you. It'd be against the law, unless you were dumb enough to spill about our plan."

"Not a word," Paul says. "Honest." His buddy doesn't look convinced, so he crosses his heart twice, hopes to die. "I swore up and down I never saw you take any coat."

"Nice to hear you didn't rat at least. Not that it makes any difference."

121

"How'd you know I didn't take anything?"

"You kidding me? When I wasn't getting slapped around in that room, I could hear you whining to the other guard who was holding you. Telling him what a good little boy you were." Hal makes a crybaby face, mimics Paul's pleading with the man to let him go. "Always figured you might chicken out the last minute."

"You should've too, then you—"

"Too late now," Hal says like it's no big deal.

Paul fights a strong urge to shake him. "So where've you been? Two weeks is a long time for a kid to disappear." He lies down facing his buddy, less worried the boy might bolt for some mysterious reason.

Hal turns on his side. He tucks an arm under his pillow, the same pillow he used during his sleepover a few short months ago. The pillow Paul hugs while asleep. "Been staying with a guy. Some old guy. Like in his 50's or more. I met him after I split the store. He lives on a little side street off Broad. Right across from the 280 access ramp before you get downtown. I hung out under that damn ramp a long time after I escaped, thinking what to do next. Freezing my ass off. I sure as hell couldn't go home. So this guy. He kept watching me from his window across the street. Had a big smile on that droopy puss of his. He called me over. We talked a while. Then he asked if I wanted to come inside."

"That was nice of him," Paul says. "Was it?"

"Real nice." Hal doesn't sound like he means it.

"Where'd you go after that?"

"Ain't no after that. It's where I'm staying for now."

"This guy live all by himself?"

"Except for me. The place is a big boarding house. He's got a room on the first floor. His own john and a little kitchen. I got to keep out of sight when the landlord collects the weekly rent from everyone, or checks on things. And he checks a lot. The building's real old, full of characters."

"Your friend a character too?" Paul says.

"He likes to make me feel good."

"Make you feel good?"

"I lie on my back, like I am now, and he blows me. That's what he wants in return for all the food I can eat. A safe place to stay until I move on."

Safe. Paul thought he understood the word before tonight. His head slides off his hand. It rests against his pillow. He gazes at his buddy as if examining a stranger. Though more beautiful than ever, Hal seems pale. Thinner too. His large brown eyes have lost their glow, the sense that someone's there behind them. It's as if he's become a kind of alien, like in sci-fi movies. The ones where people get taken over, replaced by twin versions of themselves until they're saved by the people who love them—or not.

And what does he do all day without going to school, having to stay in hiding? From what Paul's learned so far, he'd rather not ask. He gets off his bed, starts to pace. He needs to be in motion.

"Got ants in your pants?" Hal says.

"Just nervous."

"I know how to calm you down."

"That's not a good idea."

"Since when? Since I told you about—"

"The guard at the store," Paul says. "The one who hit you. It was all self-defense what you did. You were protecting yourself from a grown man. My mom said so."

"Your mom?"

"After you ran off, the cops came to the store and took me down the station. They called my dad. I was there a long time getting grilled by a detective about you, and yelled at by my old man for hanging out with you when he told me not to."

"What'd you tell them about me?"

"Same thing I told the store guard who held me. The detective kept wanting me to fink on you. But I swore I never saw you steal anything, and that we never planned to. I kept going back instead to how the guard beat you up. That was something the cop didn't want to hear.

"My dad drove me home after I got released. Him and Mom and me talked about everything that happened. We talked a long time. I got another big lecture but that was all. And I kept waiting for shit to hit the fan. Somewhere around the end my mom said, for like the hundredth time, what you did was very wrong. The stealing, I mean. But she thought that the guard never should've hit you like that. She said he was in a lot more trouble than you. My dad didn't think so. He said the guard probably was defending himself. He said you got what you deserved. They almost had a big argument. But he's nosing around to move back in soon and let it drop."

"So what're you telling me? I should give myself up because your old lady thinks I might get off?"

"Didn't mean that exactly."

"What did you mean exactly?" Hal springs up and hauls Paul back onto the mattress, straddling him. He bends low. So low his face almost becomes a blur. His breath is hot and dry. "What if I told you I'd do whatever you want? Put my frigging life in your hands? But before you start shelling out dumb advice, remember I got priors. I could get a long rap in some reform school."

Hal's question overwhelms Paul. The responsibility it carries. More than anything he wants his buddy's mess smoothed over, made right. Wants Hal back home and away from that man. But what if Lenora's wrong? What does she know about anything except soap operas, much less how the law works? "Never mind," he says. "I was only wishing. But what'll you do otherwise? You can't keep living where you're at now. And you can't quit school."

"Ain't going to. I'll be leaving soon. I can go to school in Syracuse."

Always There by Leaving

"Where's that?"

"Upstate New York. I got family there. A stepbrother. He's older than me and Ritchie. Like ten years older. He kicked around the country a lot when he was just a kid. Got in trouble too. So he knows the score. Gonna take me in and get me resettled. I called him from a pay phone a few nights after it happened. Told him everything."

"I didn't even know you had another brother. You never said."

"Never had to." Hal scratches his torso, rubs his head like he's washing it, running long fingers through wavy brown hair that looks black in the weak light. He gets off Paul, lands softly on the floor. He almost loses his balance. "Man, I'm thirsty. And I got to use the john." He reaches for the doorknob.

"Let me check first." Paul sticks his head out the door. The kitchen nightlight casts the room in dramatic shadows. A faint glow reaches the parlor. He can make out a few branches of the spruce tree, the easy chair moved to accommodate it.

"Make me wait any longer and I'll pee out a window."

"Okay, okay. Just stay quiet." Paul follows his buddy into the kitchen, hands him a plastic cup from the dish rack. "Drink in there."

With Hal in the john, Paul steals into the parlor. He makes his way to his mother's bedroom at the other end. He presses his ear to where the sliding doors meet, hears a

126

buzz, more like purring static. Lenora must've fallen asleep with the TV on. No wonder she didn't hear his buddy's clumsy entrance. Meanwhile, the flushing sound from the toilet seems endless. The bathroom door creaks open.

Hal walks into the parlor despite being signaled not to.

"Go back to my room," Paul says.

Hal ignores him. He stares at the Christmas tree as if mesmerized. He gets down on all fours, paws his way around the red-and-glitter felt wrapped along the base. Some tinsel gets stuck in his hair along the back of his head. He doesn't seem to notice.

Paul kneels beside him. "What're you doing?"

"Where's the plug? I want to see the lights on."

"You what?"

"Found it."

Paul stays his hand.

"Said I want to see the damn tree."

Paul envisions the two of them in a reckless struggle to control the cord. The tree topples down in a tangled mess. A mess Lenora didn't create.

"Let me check my mom first." He feels the tension in Hal's arm diminish. He hears a terse okay and hops into action, not wanting to test his buddy's patience. Inch by inch, he slides open one of the heavy doors. Lenora's fast asleep. Her head resembles an artificial flower with all those blue rollers on it. Across from her the TV's gone dark. White noise pours from its speaker in a steady, soothing tone. He shuts the door and rejoins his buddy on the floor.

Hal rubs his hands together. "Here we go." He connects the extension cord. The tree lights blaze in a flash that dazzles up close.

"They'll bubble once they get warm."

"Never saw this kind before." Hal notices three boxes full of ornaments, the boxes Paul found in the closet. He reaches for one.

"Careful," Paul says. "They're glass. Real thin and old. They belonged to my great-grand parents. I wasn't allowed to handle them until we got the floor rug put in."

Hal removes an angel from its tissue paper. The robed figure is designed as a bell. Stuck together, the cherub's tiny feet serve as the clapper. He runs a finger across the ornament's translucent wings. "I could use a pair of these right now. Let's do some."

"Are you kidding?" Paul thumbs at Lenora's bedroom.

"I didn't get to do my tree this year. That's the best part of Christmas." Hal sounds plaintive as a five-year-old, his stubbornness suddenly gone. His eyes are bright and shiny, the irises like melted chocolate. He seems really back again.

Paul can't resist. "Maybe you can do one box until the lights bubble."

He knows they'll start up soon. He watches his buddy hang the ornaments in the same thoughtful manner the boy makes a drawing—or picks a lock. Hal's moves are delicate. He seems calm, content. In the multi-colored glow he's so beautiful, seems so fragile, Paul feels emptied out with admiration. He hates to break the silence, but there are things he needs to know. Hal may have to steal away at any moment, down the back stairs and out his life. Perhaps forever. The thought unsteadies him. He takes a deep breath. "When you plan on leaving?"

"Day after Christmas. Traffic should be light then, Ralph thinks. He's giving me a ride far as Kingston. I'll meet up with my brother there."

"Who's Ralph?"

"Who I'm staying with." Hal looks at Paul and seems to read his mind. "He's an okay enough guy."

Paul nods and changes the subject. "Your mom know?"

"About Ralph?"

"No." And if she does, he doesn't want to hear. "About your brother and Syracuse and all."

"Johnny called a good buddy of his down here. He got word to her."

"What's your dad think?" Paul has to wait for an answer.

"He didn't come back from his last truck run. Just stayed in Ohio. Somewhere near Cleveland. My mom thinks he's shacking up with someone. He sent me the ten bucks I showed Leon. Stuck it in a little card that said he was sorry, that he'd write why later."

129

"You never told me."

"Who says you got to know everything? Hey, the lights. They're starting to bubble." Hal watches as they pick up steam. He points to a dormant cluster. "These guys ain't working."

"Tap them lightly on the candle part. That'll wake them."

Hal's touch soon gets them going. "Now they're perfect."

"Time to quit."

"There's not that many ornaments left. Let's do the rest."

"You're making me nuts."

"You were nuts when I met you. I made you better."

"And now you're going away."

"Yeah, well." Hal proffers another box of ornaments and together they finish. He looks at their work from every angle, as if he were trying to absorb the glittering tree with his eyes, or sink into it. He yawns and stretches. "I need to lie down before I head out. Got a long walk back."

Paul hesitates answering. He wants more time with Hal, wants to forestall the agony of goodbye. But he better not press their luck. It's after three in the morning. The sooner his buddy leaves, the better.

"It's okay, ain't it?" Hal says.

"Sure. But only for a little while, you know, because."

"I know." Hal stuffs his hands in his pockets, gazes at his feet. He seems even sadder next to the festive tree.

Paul takes his buddy by the shoulders and rubs them

lightly. The gesture becomes an embrace. He could stay this way until his legs gave out. But he has to think for two. "We need to turn out the lights." He watches Hal take a final, lingering look at the tree before pulling the plug. He lets his eyes adjust to the dimness, turns back to Lenora's room. Maybe he should risk a second look and turn off her TV. Then again, the abrupt silence might awaken her. "You know when they start broadcasting again?"

"Who?"

"The morning shows on TV." Paul nods at his mother's door.

"I'll be long gone before that."

CHAPTER 9

THE HEAVY SLEET that hits the tar roof sounds like corn popping in a hot pan. Half awake, his arm draped around his buddy, the first thing Paul sees in the dark room is the back of Hal's head. He presses his nose against the boy's nape, enjoys its warm toasty smell. His left arm's numb from resting his head on it. He can't get himself to move. Not yet. Why should he? Only been a few minutes. At most a half hour since they lay down together. But then he notices the fluorescent hands of the clock atop his bureau. An icy feeling coats his gut. He climbs out of bed and listens at his door. He shakes his buddy hard, has to dodge a slow, reflexive swing.

"What the fuck?" Hal's eyes are half shut and puffy.

"Keep your voice down. It's late. I mean it's morning. You got to get out before—" Paul hears music. Military music, coming from the front of the apartment. "That's her set."

"Her what?"

"My mom's TV. It's going to wake her."

Hal fumbles out of bed. Good thing he conked out with most of his clothes on. It seems to take forever just to get his shoes and coat on.

Paul peeks out his room in time to see Lenora's door sliding open. He shuts his own. "Get in the closet. No, this one."

The closet's not as wide as the other but deeper. Like an animal prowling jungle growth, Hal cuts a path between shoes and boxes and hanging clothes. His commotion tips over the baseball bat Paul grabbed for defense last night when he feared a monster invasion. Before Paul can catch it, the bat lands on linoleum. It bounces a few times.

"Paulie?" Lenora says from the kitchen. "What was that?"

"What?"

"What do you mean 'what'?"

"My baseball bat."

"In December?"

"It got in my way last night when I was looking for the Christmas ornaments. Forgot to put it back."

Finger to lips, he signals Hal to stay quiet. He rearranges the hanging clothes to give the boy cover, shuts him in as Lenora barges in, something she's done a few times since his shoplifting mess, as if she were a prison guard pulling surprise inspections. She frowns at the bat leaning against the bureau. "Damn TV woke me up."

"I heard," he says.

"From here? Christ, you're like a dog."

"Was coming out the bathroom."

"That's where I'm heading, then back to bed." She stops

133

at the door. "The tree, by the way, it turned out nice. You did a good job."

"Yeah, *we* did."

She offers a tired smile and pads away. Once she's in the john he keeps his door ajar so he can hear. He opens the closet where his buddy sits on an old trunk jammed against the back wall.

"That was close," Hal says and gets up.

"Stay put."

"Why?"

"You heard her. She's going back to bed. Be safer then. A sure thing."

"I'm getting stir-crazy in here." Hal shrugs off his coat, folds it in his lap. "Don't like tight places."

"Won't be long."

"Better not or I'll split in front of her. What's she going to do?"

"Help my father kill me."

"Okay, okay," Hal says.

Paul gives him a quizzical look.

"What's the matter now?"

"Sometimes I think part of you wants to get caught."

"You really do got a screw loose." But Hal's blush is obvious even in the closet.

The bathroom pipes start working. Paul shuts his scowling buddy in again.

Lenora stops for a glass of water. Ankles crossed, she

leans against the sink while she sips, her eyes barely open. "Your father's coming for dinner tonight."

"I know."

"I'm fixing him something special."

"Sounds good."

"Don't you want to know what it is?"

"Tripe," Paul says. "You told me yesterday."

"It's a lot of work. Not sure I feel up to it. There's so much to do with Christmas coming, and your father moving in next week."

"Dad's moving in? When'd you decide that?"

"Last night, before I fell asleep. Maybe it was that TV show. When I woke up I felt the same way. But don't let on. I want to tell him myself."

"I won't say a word."

"We'll have Christmas as a family, the way we used to."

Paul's tight smile freezes in place. He doesn't need a mirror to know it looks phony. Why is she telling him now when she's half asleep? He should say more, show enthusiasm, but he can't take the risk. What if Hal makes a noise? What if he carries out his dumb threat and saunters out the bedroom in front of bleary-eyed Lenora? "You look real tired," he says. "We should talk about Dad's moving in later, after you've slept more. I can help with the tripe. I watched Grandma make it."

"Her tripe's different. Mine's spicier."

"But it's still tripe."

"It sure is," she says like she means something else. She refills her glass and heads out the gloomy kitchen. "Wake me up at nine. And no loud TV before."

Soon as Paul opens the closet door Hal shoves the hanging clothes aside, jumps over the floor clutter as if he were escaping a burning room. He's flustered. His breathing's heavy. He sits on the bed huffing. "She took her damn sweet time. What were you two doing in there, going through Santa's list?"

"You're out now." Paul sits beside his buddy and rubs his back.

"My shirttail's coming loose."

"Want me to stop?"

"Didn't say that."

With a deft hand, Paul tucks in the boy's shirt, noting again the thin waist. "That guy been feeding you enough?"

"I should get moving." Hal brushes away the hand.

Paul grabs the black umbrella hanging in his closet and hands it over. "It's snowing kind of heavy now. Take my galoshes too," he says recalling the hole in his buddy's shoe.

"My dogs won't fit in yours."

"They're loose on me. And they can stretch a lot."

"My head hurts when I bend over."

"Sit back and I'll do it." With some effort, and a long-handled shoehorn, Paul manages to slip the galoshes on. He opens his bedroom door and checks out the flat. He nods an okay and they walk through the kitchen to the back door. Hal makes a sudden U-turn to the sink, uses Lenora's glass to get himself some water. "Be right back." He disappears into the john. Paul stands guard, teeth clenched and counting the seconds. His own head aches from the tension.

Hallway stairs creak as the boys wend their way down in the dark. They linger at the bottom in the small, unheated vestibule.

"So this is it," Hal says.

Paul shuffles his feet on the worn tiles. "Any idea if you might be coming back sometime?"

Hal shrugs, his grim expression barely visible.

"That's okay." Paul starts to shiver from the cold.

"Should've grabbed yourself a coat."

"Yeah, I should've."

"This'll help." Hal gives him a rough, long hug that Paul melts into, his mouth against the other boy's neck, his chin resting on the stolen suede coat that ruined everything. He holds tight, won't let go. His buddy has to make that move.

"Your address for up in Syracuse. I never got it from you."

"Don't have anything to write with."

"I'll get something. Be right back."

Paul climbs the stairs and sprints to the kitchen wall phone. He grabs a pad and pen Lenora keeps on the nearby cabinet. His descent is more cautious. He rounds the curve and almost trips. There's daylight at the bottom. The vestibule is empty. He runs down the narrow alley. Out on the street to his left and well into the distance, he sees a thin, lone figure with a black umbrella walking fast in the snow. A figure that never turns around no matter how much he wills it.

Part II

Four Years Later

CHAPTER 10

PAUL TURNS HIS bike off the graveled path and onto thick grass. He settles himself beneath a huge beech tree edged on one side by thick bushes, a cool escape from bright May sunlight. Few visitors come to this isolated area of the park. Those who make the hilly trek, usually solo adults, seem more serious, as if on a mission rather than a stroll. They walk with purpose, arms swinging. Paul can imagine fife-and-drum music whenever one passes. He collects a jumbo canteen and his book assignment from the bike's wire basket. He leans against the tree's smooth bark. It's a perfect spot for reading *Siddhartha*.

The warm canteen water has a metallic tang. In the still air he smells new grass and shaded soil. He's grateful the novel features large type. Another kid assigned the same book in a prior semester underlined the most important stuff. Paul doesn't need the accidental help. He's relishing the story. Maybe someday he'll travel to India during the coolest month of winter, when that country's not a furnace or flooded with a monsoon. Jersey summers are hot and wet enough.

Summer. This coming summer. The collision course with his father. He has to stand firm this time. Has too.

He wrestles the subject from his mind and loses himself

in the book. About an hour passes, along with the occasional visitor. A squeaking sound distracts him, one that doesn't come from birds or park animals. It's a bike with a noisy train struggling up the path. No wonder. The blond boy riding it is too large for the small cycle. He pedals like a circus clown, his fat knees and long feet spread wide, his bloated expression determined, grim, suffused with red. Above the struggling boy, atop the hill opposite Paul, there stands a barrel-chested man. He stares down his aquiline nose watching the young rider's progress. His massive round head doesn't move. With his small dark eyes, russet skin and spiked black hair, he could be an Indian—the American kind. Paul imagines the stranger in feathered headdress and buckskin. He's toting a bow and arrow. A golden horse stands beside him, alert, faithful. Like in the movies.

Slowly the boy and his bicycle move from sight. The man stays. His gaze shifts to Paul. His large, symmetrical features form a kind of crosshairs. He smiles. At least he seems to. But those twisted ripples of flesh can't be a smile. Not with eyes that seem to glow hot as he descends the hill, his pace casual, not once looking down to check his footing. He opens his mouth as if to speak, but doesn't. He's too far away for that.

But already much too close for Paul. He grabs his canteen and makes for his bike. The man's amble turns to a clumsy sprint. His corrugated smile mutates into something more frightening. Flanked on one side by thick bushes,

Paul's only escape is the path. If he doesn't act soon the man's approach will block his flight downhill. Maybe it's too late already. Maybe he should abandon the heavy red bike and hope his legs can carry him upwards fast enough to safety. He decides on a gamble. With the bike beside him, he runs along the lumpy ground and thick grass towards the descent, where the man also makes tracks. Once his wheels hit the path he jumps on his ride and puts on speed. The man races close behind. Paul hears feet pounding gravel; hears raspy breathing and words shouted at him, angry words in another language. A glance back slows his momentum. It's enough for his pursuer to make a grab for the bike's fender. He swerves right and barely evades reach. He'd go faster if he could keep his legs steady. His trembling causes one foot to slip from its pedal. He almost loses control, manages to stay upright in time to veer left and dodge another close call.

Further down where the terrain becomes level he sees teenaged boys. More than a dozen in all. They approach the path from a field. He expects them to keep his way clear while he races along. They crowd the trail instead, make him wheel onto the grass.

"Who do you think you are?" one kid says.

"You better slow down or else," another warns.

Other boys join in. They shout vague, garbled threats.

"This big guy's chasing me," Paul yells back. "He came from nowhere. He wants to kill me or something—I swear." The boys look at each other, then past Paul. In an instant their anger shifts to his pursuer. Kids with bats split from the group. They start swinging their clubs, their faces menacing, eager.

"The fucker's running the other way," a boy shouts over triumphant jeering. He signals it's safe to slow down and stop. Paul does. He skids a little from applying the foot break too hard. He's yards from the group. Now that he's stopped he finds he can't move anymore, can't get enough air in his lungs. The boys gather around him. He thanks them again and again in between breaths.

"He all gone yet?"

"See for yourself," one tells him.

"Shouldn't we get the cops?" His question provokes a rambling debate. His eyes can't seem to focus on any one boy. Their faces remain a blur.

"Forget the cops," someone says from the back. "Too late for those clowns to do anything."

"But what about another kid?" Paul says.

"That'll be his lookout." The boy with the deep voice giving advice works his way to the front, where the tallest kids stand. Paul stares at him, head cocked.

"Hey, Paulie. Long time no see."

Paul only can nod. He fights off a sudden urge to south-paw the grinning boy.

"Didn't recognize you at first," Hal says. "You got even uglier."

The other kids look at Paul, waiting for his response.

"Got a long way to catch up with you."

It's a lame retort. But Hal laughs. So do the other boys, their expressions curious, alert.

"Mind if I stick with you guys a while?" Paul doesn't have to explain, doesn't need to wait for agreement. He's made welcome with few words. He falls in with them as they walk.

Several question him about the man who chased him. He has little to tell. When he's done, a few kids share their narrow escapes from danger. The stories differ from his in situation. A fire. A car accident. A close encounter with boiling hot water. He listens without looking at Hal, who's drifted to the periphery. Boys start to drop away from the large group, head for different routes out the park. Their goodbyes are short. Some make plans to meet up later after dinner, or on Sunday. He notices no one goes off alone. They leave in two's and three's. He and Hal remain. Plus a couple skinny guys named Rick and Manny. Their voices and dark, comely features are so alike, they must be brothers.

His eyes meet Hal's. "You heading out to Summer Ave?"

"Don't live there no more."

Paul waits for more info but doesn't get any. "Is it a big secret?"

"What?"

"Don't play dumb. Are you still living in Syracuse? You here on a visit or something?"

Hal looks annoyed.

"You never told us you lived in Syracuse," Rick says. "Where's that?"

"Pennsylvania," his brother says. "Right?"

"Right," Hal tells him, "Close to Pittsburgh."

Manny seems pleased with himself. Paul doesn't let on. He hopes Hal might walk with him without the other boys. "Where you going now?"

"Not sure yet." Hal picks up the copy of *Siddhartha* from Paul's bike basket. The cover art features the Buddha as a beautiful, androgynous youth with long black hair and brown skin. He sits cross-legged under an enormous tree. His lithe body seems to hover above the ground. Hal tosses the book into the basket. He turns his back to Paul in a way that feels like a snub. "You guys want to do the Space Tree?"

The brothers seem unsure at first, and then agree. Paul waits to get asked, but doesn't.

"What about him? I think we can trust him." Manny turns to his brother.

"Yeah. He kind of owes us."

"Fine with me," Hal says. "Just figured he'd want to get home to Mommy and Daddy."

"I'm okay."

"Sure you are. That's why you haven't moved your ass off that bike."

146

Paul shrugs. It was awkward to walk while sitting on his cycle, but he felt safer on it, ready to flee.

"You can't ride there," Manny tells him. "The tree ain't nowhere near a regular path. And it's a secret. Only a few other kids know."

"I won't tell. But why's it special?"

"You don't find out unless you come," Hal says.

"That figures. You haven't changed much after all." Paul shifts his body, tries to dismount. His limbs stay locked in place. Embarrassed, he tries again. His right leg swings up, but not enough to pass the saddle. He loses his balance and almost topples.

Hal grabs the handle bars and straddles the front wheel. He holds the red bike for Paul to dismount. "I'll walk it for you until you're steady."

Paul nods okay. He reaches for his canteen. It's still quite full. He passes it around as they quit the path for a hill obscured by thickets and low-hanging cherry blossom trees. Beyond them lies a heavily wooded area that includes the narrow river. The quartet splits into pairs. Unencumbered by the bike Manny and Rick walk ahead. They recap the afternoon ballgame, critique the other players good naturedly. Sometimes they finish each other's sentences. Rick hikes up his pants often to keep them from sliding past narrow hips.

"Does he do that when he's running bases?" Paul asks.

"He's a good little player," Hal says.

"Didn't mean otherwise. As for little, he's taller than you are. Me too, by a couple inches or more."

"So what?"

"So it's been a long time's all I'm saying. Since I saw you I mean."

"Couldn't be helped."

"Could've been helped the *way* you left. What kind of friend does that?" And it's like the four years since that morning never passed. Paul's back on his snowy winter street, watching his buddy in the distance walk away on the sly.

Hal stops short and gives him a swift once-over. "You're doing okay now." He releases the bike. Paul grabs his ride before it tips over. They glare at each other until Manny and Rick, well ahead, turn around and shout at them to get a move on.

The serpentine footpath, long neglected, narrows as the quartet treks further up the hill. It's essential they walk single file. Slowed by his ride Paul trails last, behind Hal, who hasn't spoken to him since handing over the bike. Rick and Manny continue talking baseball. They move onto professional teams and Hal joins in. The trio considers a dizzying array of stats from the prior season, stats the two brothers seem to know by heart, but Paul only half understands. He never can remember what all the acronyms mean. Whenever Rick or Manny asks his opinion, he takes the majority view. Then he throws the question back about the first player who comes to mind, one mentioned earlier in passing, and hopes they don't catch on, realize he has little idea what he's talking about.

And so it goes until the boys come to a high ridge, one that overlooks a slender gulley with a steep drop. Jagged grooves scar the brown earth below. Grass and weeds form a sparse covering. It's as if a giant bear had clawed the land in search of food and left a deep hole. Close to the center a single tree, a towering sycamore, dominates the chasm. A long cable is tied to the tree's thickest branch. The remains of an aborted landscaping project, the cable extends in the air and up to the ridge, where it's tethered with a noose to a sturdy bush.

"Here it is," Rick says, "The Space Tree!"

Paul checks out the cable attached to the sycamore.

"Bet I know what this is for."

"It's rusted more over the winter," Rick tells him. "We got to be careful about splinters. They can dissolve in your skin. That's what I heard somewhere. Otherwise it's real easy and the best fun ever."

"Not if you're Paulie," Hal says. "He's chicken-shit of heights."

"I was never more scared than you. Just a lot less dumb about taking a risk."

"Then you show us how to do it, smart guy."

"But he hasn't done it before," Manny says.

"Neither did you your first try."

"Yeah, but you taught us."

"Nobody taught me."

"Hal always knows what to do," Paul says. "That's why he never gets in any trouble."

"Enough already," Rick says. "I'll go first."

He reaches into Paul's bike basket for the canteen and takes a long drink. He rolls his shoulders in their thin sockets. He and Manny slip the cable from the bush. Manny leans back, tugs the noose low as it'll go so his brother can get his right leg into it up to his buttock. Rick grabs the cable with both hands. Manny holds him at the waist to keep him from getting dragged off the ridge.

"Must be heavier than it looks," Paul says.

"And hard to control when you want to stop," Rick tells him. "You lose all your whatchamacallit. Someone's got to break you after you hit the ground. Otherwise you might sail right back."

"How'd you do it alone?" Paul asks.

"Swung in sideways," Hal says, "Then I backed into the bush and let it stop me."

"That must've hurt."

"I had a coat on."

"Was it a suede coat like the one you got yourself for Christmas?"

Hal's shoulders tense. His hands form fists. He looks like he might take a swing. He may not have grown as much in height, but he's a lot more muscular. His face distorts with anger. He walks up to Paul like a boot-camp sergeant about chew out a recruit. "Why don't you go read your book somewhere?"

"Or maybe I should go first. How hard can it be if a guy like you can do it?"

"Maybe you should." Hal backs off, all smiles

Paul can't believe he let himself get baited like that. Who's the dumbbell now? But he had to do something big in front of the other boys. He saw questions in their eyes or thought he did. Painful questions best to avoid in the middle of nowhere.

He walks to the ridge and scans the deep gulley.

"Forget about going first," Rick tells him. "I'll show you how."

"And I'm tired of holding him," Manny says.

"So go already," Hal says as if he were in charge. "The bookworm can go next, unless he punks out again."

"Why don't you tell them about the time I punked out and you didn't? I bet they'd like to hear what happened to you."

The brothers ignore the verbal sparring. Rick leans back far as he can. He lifts his feet off the ground and coils his legs tight while Manny lets go. He yodels like Tarzan. His slender body races to the bottom, only to ascend with such momentum he seems in danger of going full circle. How small and helpless he looks at the furthest distance, until he grows larger swinging back to the ridge, only to go out again, laughing and hooting like a little kid on a park swing.

"You're way past the limit," Hal says. "Give someone else a chance."

"Like your brother," Manny says.

Rick takes a few more swings before he signals he's ready. He's going fast. Manny and Hal help him land.

"You always go nuts on that thing," Manny gripes.

"It's good training."

"For what?" Paul says.

"I want to be a professional skydiver."

"Your turn," Hal says. "Unless you want to—"

"I don't," Paul says. "I mean I'm ready."

"Someone better help me out of this."

Hal and Manny bookend Rick. The boy wraps his arms around their shoulders. He slips his leg out the noose without dragging it across the cable's rough surface. He has a wobbly walk now that he's earthbound. Elated by his ride he beams at Paul. "Takes a minute to get your stride back."

"I'm sure it does."

"Time to find out for yourself." Hal holds the noose in place.

"You look like a hangman in a Western."

"No one's forcing you."

"Give the cable to Rick and Manny. Them I trust."

Paul's installation goes well. The brothers are careful

and methodical. They give plenty of tips on what he should do once he's off the ledge, dependent on the coiled steel and the sycamore's muscular branch, which appears much less strong from his new perspective. He nods at their advice, but only half listens. He wonders if the other boy's ride may have weakened the wood. Didn't he hear a creaking sound while Rick was going at it? Just looking up at the branch makes him dizzy. What'll happen once he's in flight, high above the ground, racing toward the other side? What if he blacks out? Or loses his grip? No matter what he's determined to go past the limit—twenty swings, isn't it?—to show he's enjoying himself and can run the distance.

Meanwhile Rick's embrace feels good against his waist. It's been so long since another boy touched him like that. Not since Hal, who stands to the side, a smug expression on his face, like he's waiting for a punk-out.

"What're you smirking at?"

"Someone got awful pale. And what's with the shaky legs all of a sudden?"

"Guess they want to kick ass."

"In your dreams."

"You're fine," Rick tells him. "But you don't have to."

"Yeah," Manny says.

"Are you kidding? I'm looking forward to it."

Manny rests a hand on Paul's shoulder. "It sounds crazy, but if you close your eyes while you're riding, it don't seem half as scary. And it ain't like you got to see where you're going. The cable takes you there anyway."

"But then you miss all the fun," Rick says. "And I didn't know you closed your eyes."

"Only my first time, in the beginning."

"Is this a fucking history class?" Hal says.

"I'll let you go on ten." Rick says.

"Make it five," Hal tells him.

Rick draws out the count, probably to allow for a last-second change of heart. He seems that kind of kid. His voice is soft, but to Paul it sounds like a rubber hammer striking iron. Already his knuckles are white and sore from clenching the cable.

"Five!" Rick yells and leaves go.

Paul follows Manny's advice and closes his eyes, but he finds blindness too disorienting. And he's sure it weakens his grip somehow. He keeps his eyes open the second time, focused on the opposite ridge, the line of trees there, and the winding river that blends with the horizon and the sky filled with white clouds. His third time out he lets himself enjoy the strong sexual pleasure he felt from the beginning, but suppressed for fear of losing control. With each swing the sensation builds to a more insistent level. The other boys cheer him on. Rick and Manny do anyway. Their voices deliver a welcome distraction. They keep him set on his flight, lift him with supportive words. His efforts seem so easy now, he'd like to abandon the harness and levitate in midair, like the beautiful brown Siddhartha. If this is what enlightenment feels like, he's ready for the journey. He aims higher, then higher still.

At the bottom of his swing, gliding backwards toward his launching pad, the cable loses all its tension. The noose that supports him no longer presses against his buttock. Instinctively he lets go. He falls so fast he's on the ground before he knows what happened. The long cable follows after like a giant snake about to pounce. Frozen in place he shuts his eyes, fearing the worse. He hears a loud crumbling sound to his left. He looks up, glad to see the tree branch intact. He seems bodiless, a pair of eyes rooted in the earth. It's not a bad feeling.

Hal arrives before the brothers, his face a mass of worry. He runs his hands all over Paul. "You okay?" he keeps asking and "Are you hurt?" and "Can you talk?" and "I'm sorry, Paulie, I'm sorry," then back to "You okay?" until Paul finally mumbles something.

The brothers arrive in a commotion of footsteps. "How is he?" Manny says.

"Can you move?" Rick says.

Paul shrugs.

"That's good for starters. Can you move everything else?"

"We got to get the cable off him first," Hal says.

The boys remove Paul's leg from the noose. Slowly he spreads his limbs as if he were trying to make a timid snow angel on the bare ground. He looks up, sees three relieved faces.

"He can move," Manny says. "That means he's not—"

"Shut up," Hal says. "How's your neck and your head? You feeling dizzy?"

Paul shakes his head. The boys lift him to his feet and hold fast until he can stand alone. Stiff legged, feeling no pain, he looks around, confused by the new perspective.

"You want to try walking?" Hal wraps his arm around the boy's waist. Paul does the same to him. The two walk a while this way.

"I'm okay," Paul says. "Let's get out of here."

They trudge up the ridge holding each other. Rick and Manny follow, chattering about Paul's miraculous drop and all the bad things that could've happened, but didn't.

CHAPTER 11

NOT FAR FROM the park, Rick and Manny say their hasty goodbyes outside Whitey's Corner Shop on Mt. Prospect. They're eager to get home and eat. Much as he likes them Paul's glad to see the brothers go, leaving him alone with Hal. There's so much he needs to know and tell.

Hal wants to buy him lunch on account of his mishap. The offer makes him happy at first. Then he worries where the money came from. It's a reflexive concern, one he puts aside while Hal secures the bike to a traffic sign, the bike he insisted on walking ever since they left the Space Tree. His slowness with the tricky lock makes Paul nervous. He doesn't want his father or any of Max's club friends seeing them together.

The street corner, part of a small commercial hub, is close to home. It can get busy on Saturdays. He's on the lookout for familiar faces. His eyes jump from the redbrick factory where cardboard boxes are made, to Mandy's discount clothing store with its spring sale, to Landsman's Pharmacy, then further down the avenue to Parillo's hardware store that always smells of fresh plywood, and gets mostly men as customers. Some old people in flats above the stores sit at their windows. Their sagging expressions are vacant, pale and unmoving. They recall eerie, nineteenth-century photographs of dead people, where the deceased, eyes open, are propped in sitting positions, made to appear alive. Paul's favorite art teacher showed the pictures in class one day.

The narrow, smoky luncheonette reeks of cooking grease. There's a cloying sweetness from grilled onions and badly lidded ketchup jars. A stooped, gray-haired man prepares a malted milk at a yellow Formica counter. Dishes and pots clatter from behind the small serving hatch that opens to the kitchen. The lunch rush, if there was one, has past. Some diners sit at the counter. A few read one of the sensational tabloids sold at the shop. Others sip their coffee, listen to the radio heard over the buzzing green blender. All the middle-aged customers are strangers. Paul can relax a little.

They duck into the tiny bathroom together and clean up.

The counter guy spots Hal when they come out. His wide smile stretches across tobacco-stained teeth.

"How's about some table service, Whitey?"

"Be right with you, kid."

"Get us two colas to start."

Whitey uses extra-large glasses for the drinks, which he pours from a fountain. He sets them on the counter. He barely acknowledges Paul, who makes for a back table before Hal insists on another setup. This one at a picture window near the entrance. The cash register opposite them is framed with confection shelves in front and cigarette racks behind. Candy wrappers glitter like jewels in the afternoon sun.

"We better keep an eye on your bike," Hal says. "I opened that lock twice without the key."

Paul's heart races at the show of concern. "So that's what took you so long. For a minute I thought you lost your touch."

"Once you got it..." Hal blows on his square fingertips and rubs them against his plaid shirt. The sleeves are rolled halfway up his forearms. A hard smile reshapes his taut skin and then disappears, leaving no sign the smile happened or was genuine. He turns to the window. In profile he looks even more young man than boy. The striking maturity captivates Paul, who's grateful his own view to the street is interrupted by faded posters taped to glass. They offer him some cover. He dumps his book and canteen on the empty chair behind him.

"It's a beauty, isn't it?"

"I'm past bikes myself," Hal says. "Saving all my scratch for a set of wheels like that."

Paul watches the sleek black car pull away from the traffic light. "You need big money to buy a Thunderbird."

"You're shitting me." Hal pulls a shocked expression and they both laugh. His face seems the same, but different. A shadow of beard runs completely from ear-to-ear. His nose is longer, thicker, less upturned, as if resculpted.

Thank goodness no one's broken it yet. The scar on his neck. That's new as well. Thin and straight, like someone marked the flesh with stark white chalk.

Paul touches his own neck, resting two fingertips on his pulse.

"Knife fight," Hal says.

"What?"

"Don't pretend. You're still lousy at it."

"Did it happen in Syracuse?"

"Jersey. One of the bush boys went mental on me and surprised me from behind."

A bush boy? Paul envisions a wild, half-naked kid jumping from a tree with a machete. He waits to hear more but doesn't. He's relieved not to. He's starving and doesn't want to lose his appetite. "I got my bike the Christmas you left me for Syracuse. I mean, you left *for* Syracuse." His face grows hot. His scalp tingles. So much for playing it Joe Cool. He wants to hear about that city, so close to the Canadian border according to the colorful road map of New York State he hung on his bedroom wall, much to his mother's curiosity. He told her he liked the pyramidal shape. "What's it like up there?"

"Wasn't around long enough to find out."

"You weren't?"

"Some things happened."

"What things?"

"More like one big thing."

160

Paul takes a deep breath. "How big?" He hopes it doesn't concern knives.

Whitey reaches the table before Hal can answer. The man's a shuffler. His shoes slide over worn linoleum like a pair of leather brooms. "What'll it be fellas." He looks at Hal with anticipation that seems way overblown for a food order.

Paul grabs a cardboard menu from the clip stand. There's not much on it. Like painting swatches, the hand-written list appears to have a stain of everything available.

"The usual for me and make it pronto." Hal raps his knuckles on the table. "We've had a busy day."

"You're a regular here?" Paul can't believe the other boy's been so near at times. And for how long?

"Me and Whitey are buddies, ain't we?"

"You bet, kid. And I got another favor you can do me." The man rubs his swollen wrist.

"So what'll you have?"

"It's okay to say?" Whitey darts his eyes at Paul.

"I wasn't talking to you."

"Sure kid, sure. That's what I meant."

"I'll have whatever he's having," Paul says because it's quicker. He repeats himself so the man can listen with his good ear. "What'd I order?" he asks when they're alone.

"Good stuff."

"So what about Syracuse? Can you answer me that?"

Hal takes a long sip of cola and scans the candy display.

161

"It was on account of the school up there. After my brother got me registered, the administration sent for my records. Soon as Jersey got the request they called the cops. My records must've been flagged or something. Got my ass hauled back in a flash."

"I never heard about this," Paul says. "I never saw you in school again or anywhere else. And I looked around plenty in case things didn't work out for you up there." He kept hoping they wouldn't. He yearned for his friend's return, convinced himself Hal's righteous assault on the guard would be pardoned immediately as self-defense. For months he haunted the places where the two hung out. At first he'd say Hal's name softly, wishing the boy to materialize. Weeks passed. In the park he made a ritual of chanting the name. People took notice. Word got around to his family and, more important, to his father's buddies in the club. "What'd they do to you?" he says.

"Sent me away."

"To a reformatory?" He can't say the word jail.

"A place named Hollyfield. And it's called a residential treatment center, not a reformatory."

He glances at the scar on Hal's neck. "What was it like?"

"Out in the sticks. No walls or gates even. Lots of trees on the grounds like in a park. There's a small farm to work on, and animals you can take care of if you want. All the kids live in group cottages around a big square. The sissies

162

and crazies are kept separate from the other boys. The girls too. Most of the time anyway. I managed to sneak one into my cottage cellar whenever I got the chance. Bunny fucked her behind the furnace."

"Did you like her a lot?"

Hal pulls a face. "She was a rip, that's all. And even dumber than the O.D.s."

"Who are they?"

"Officers of the Day. Guards who work with the cottage parents to make sure kids behave and stay on the grounds. Those guys are big and tough. But talk about your dim bulbs. I managed to slime them whenever I wanted to disappear at night for a while."

"What'd you do?"

"This'n'that. A few times I hotwired a car in the closest town and went joyriding. Pretty much taught myself to drive that way. But I always returned the ride to wherever I found it."

"Ever get caught?"

"Not once."

"And you always came back?"

"You're catching on."

"But why when you could've been free? That doesn't sound like the kid I remember."

"Didn't have a place I wanted to go. Not without causing trouble for other people."

"Like your mom?"

Hal slouches in his chair. Anger hardens his face. A pout erases his growing manliness. "My second year they let me get on the home visiting program. Wanted to see my old lady since she stopped visiting. And hardly wrote. When I got home I found this creep living with her. Some alky scuzzball she never told me about. She knew what I'd think of him. What I'd think of her too. Ten minutes I'm in the place and I wanted to leave. Stayed that way the whole visit."

Paul watches him twist a napkin until it's thin as a kite string.

"How's it for you now?"

"How's what?"

"Being home, since you're back to stay."

"I'm back all right. But I ain't staying with those two. The state assigned me to a group home close to downtown. The operator's a pushover. And my caseworker's pretty much hands-off since I got out and ain't been a problem."

"Here it comes!" Whitey says like he's announcing a Thanksgiving feast. But he doesn't carry most of the food. Instead he holds a tray with small bowls on it. He shuffles far behind a wide, squat woman. She has puffy bleached hair and a heavy stride. Her hands and fleshy arms manage two oblong dinner plates. She glares at Hal as if she'd prefer to dump the food on his head.

"Mrs. B.," he says. "What an honor."

"Likewise." She serves his order.

"Think you made a mistake here, Mrs. B. The other one's mine."

She examines the plate in her hand. "They're both the same. Medium-well."

"If they were *exactly* alike there wouldn't be two. I'm sure that one's mine."

"Then switch it yourself." She slides the other dish in front of Paul without looking at him and leans into Hal. "Business is up lately. That's the only reason I don't—"

"Anna made this fresh this morning," Whitey cuts in, shuffling up behind his wife. He passes the tray for her to serve.

Hal gives his bowl of coleslaw the onceover. "Went too heavy on the mayo again, Mrs. B."

"That's because I put something special in it just for you."

"Now Anna, let me take care of the fellas."

Mrs. B. doesn't budge. She keeps smoothing her apron, stained much like the menu Paul ordered from.

Two laughing little kids, one with a bouncing cowlick, careen into the shop and head straight for the shimmering candies. They pace the shelves from end to end, gently shove each other, shouting their choices, which keep changing.

"I'll handle the check-out. You do the counter." Whitey shuffles off like it's a done deal. Mrs. B. waves a dismissive hand in the air and does an about-face. But not before warning Hal to remember what she said.

Paul stares at his cheeseburger deluxe. Except for a few more fries and one less pickle slice, he doesn't see any difference in the servings.

Hal doesn't bother to switch plates despite the fuss he made. Instead he digs into his burger, bends over the dish so the greasy juices won't drip down his wrists. Wavy brown hair falls over his forehead. He wipes his mouth with several napkins. "Come on and dig in. Don't worry about Mrs. B. She didn't put something 'special' in your chow. The old bird's got a nasty sense of humor. She don't like that some favors cost money."

Paul grabs a fry and chews. The mushy inside sticks to the back of his throat like the flour glue he used to nibble on in kindergarten. He guzzles down some soda. "Shouldn't favors be free?"

"This one's different. It's more a business favor."

Paul nods like he understands, though it's impossible to imagine Hal working in the store even for a little while. Not with Mrs. B. around. He starts on his burger. Unlike the pasty French fry, the juicy meat and melted cheese stir his voracious teenage appetite. He's starving again. One bite leads to another without interruption. He's on automatic, couldn't stop if he tried. The first burger still unfinished, he could eat a second. Maybe a third.

Hal watches with obvious enjoyment. "You're breaking a world record. Save room for dessert."

"What kind of food did you get in Holyfield?"

"*Holly*field," Hal says. "Better than I ever got before or since. And more of it. Better clothes too. No hand-me-down's that were crap to begin with. Got to choose some cool threads my first day."

Paul can't help thinking about the stolen coat. How Hal's taking it got him sent to a place that supplied nice clothes for free. Kind of. His English Lit teacher would appreciate the irony. "Did you go to school while you were there?"

"Course I did. They got all kinds of classes a kid could take. I tried most of them, including auto mechanics. That's where I figured how to hotwire cars. My last semester they let me go to a regular high school. Get me used to life outside the place. It's called community adjustment. I'm a junior now just like you."

"You make it sound like you got a better deal in Jersey then in Syracuse."

Hal looks at Paul like he's crazy. "The court didn't stick me in that place as a reward."

"You said the cops did it."

"They can't put a kid away without a court saying so. Who'd you think handed out my sentence?"

"There was a trial?"

"Now I know you're shitting me."

"But I never heard. And the detective who grilled me. He didn't call or anything. Said he would if the court got involved. Said I'd have to be a witness. I could've told them about that guard."

"I copped a plea," Hal says. "No way I was walking. Not with my record and the lawyer they threw me. Fucker kept dozing off at the arraignment. Besides I didn't want you there."

"Why not?"

"You'd've caved. Spilled all about the plan and that old gasbag, Leon. Then you'd be in trouble too even though you didn't take scratch. I told the cops I snatched the damn coat on the fly. That you didn't know shit about it. They believed me since most kids'll rat, try to blame the other guy. They didn't care about you anyway. It ain't like you whacked someone's lights out."

Paul can't think what to say. He's gratified knowing Hal wanted to protect him, if only from himself. But he's angry too. Angry he wasn't trusted enough to help. And he couldn't miss the resentment directed at him, as if he shared some blame for the outcome. He digs into Mrs. B's extra creamy coleslaw. "Where you going now?"

"After lunch?"

"I mean what school."

"Barringer."

"I'm at Arts High."

"Figures."

"And why's that?"

Hal shrugs.

"It wasn't easy getting into that school. I had to take a special test. A drawing test. And I never did much drawing before. Then I had to write an essay on the spot. After that two teachers interviewed me for what seemed like forever. It's like I was applying to a college. You should've heard my father when I told him I got accepted. He didn't want me to go. Said it was for weirdoes and beatniks and commies. My mom was okay with it. Once my doctor weighed in it was pretty much settled."

"You need a doc's okay for art school? What in hell's wrong with you?"

"Not that way. And wrong's the wrong word."

"You just used it."

"I mean he's a psychiatrist."

"Oh, a head shrinker. That figures too."

"You need to stop saying that. And he's not a 'head shrinker.' He's an amazing man. Been going to him pretty much since you left. He calls himself a Jungian—after Carl Jung. And he's a socialist too. Escaped from Hungary when the Russians pulled a big military crackdown there. They came in with tanks and stuff. He talks about himself when I can't about me. I like those sessions best. You'd like him too. He's traveled most everyplace worth going to. And he knows a lot about any subject you can think of."

"Sounds like someone's in love," Hal says.

Paul's never spoken with anyone about the doctor before. Not his family. Nor the few kids he hangs out with in school but nowhere else to avoid getting too close. For some reason he thought Hal'd understand.

169

"Maybe I am in love, kind of. Dr. Fabiani says it's okay for me to feel that way."

"How often you see this guy?"

"Twice a week."

"And you still live over that club?"

"I don't get you."

"Shrinks cost a lot of scratch. Your old man must be doing good."

"I wish. The state pays for most of it. Dr. Fabiani said so. And I'm not supposed to worry about stuff like that. It's bad for my therapy. What would you know about it anyway?"

"What don't I know. I saw a shrink every week at the center. Not because I needed to. It was something every kid had to do. Part of rehab. Saw a social worker too."

"You all rehabilitated now?"

"What do you think? And be careful how you answer."

Hal smiles like he's kidding. Paul can tell he's not.

"You seem okay enough. But then you've always been okay with me, except when you got us in trouble." His face grows hot again. He has to turn away, hears a welcome chuckle.

"Maybe you can draw me someday," Hal says.

"You'd make a good subject."

"I would?"

"The best."

"Why's that?"

"You know why."

"Remind me."

Paul briefly feels the other boy's leg brushing against his own. Is he being flirted with? He's pretty sure he is. But maybe it's only more wishful thinking. He'd like to know if Hal met a boy he really liked at Hollyfield. Or has a special buddy here in town. He's working up the nerve to ask when he spots Caputo's truck stopped at the intersection. He drops to the floor.

"What're you doing?"

"My father."

"What about him?"

"He's driving the butcher's van. He makes weekend deliveries for them." He cranes his neck, sees Hal lean close to the window, using its reflection to comb his hair as if wanting to draw attention.

"You okay kid?" From his perch at the register, Whitey's been watching his young customers—Hal especially—in between working the till.

"Think I dropped something." Paul sweats out the traffic light pretending he's on a search. He slides back in his chair and jokes about the close call and Hal's behavior. "Maybe you should've ducked too."

"Why should I give a fuck if your old man sees me? I don't answer to him."

"I was only kidding." Paul feels a strong chill from across the table. It's like they're in the park again starting from square one. He wants to get the warmth back. But how? He doesn't have time to find an answer.

"Hey, Whitey." Hal mimes writing a check.

The proprietor shuffles over fast as he can. "Lunch's on me like always. You too, kid," he tells Paul. "Now about that favor." He points a gnarled thumb to the street.

"I'm out of chewing gum," Hal says. They talk instead in front of the candy display, leaving Paul at the table. He can't hear what they're saying over the radio, not with Hal speaking low into the man's good ear and Whitey whispering back. He checks out the lunch counter. Mrs. B.'s pouring coffee for some new customers. She makes a show of cleaning up. But she keeps a bead on her husband. Her manner seems tense and hesitant. She strides to the end of the counter, making tracks for the register. Halfway there Whitey meets her gaze. His expression is pleading, desperate. His wife freezes. Eventually she retreats, her steps heavy, her face swollen with anger.

Hal takes a bunch of gum and a candy bar. He walks back to the table and slides the candy bar into Paul's shirt pocket. "Enjoy the dessert."

He's out the door straight away.

Paul can catch up with ease if he wants. Only a year ago he'd have been on his feet in a shot, ready to say anything, do anything, to get back in the other boy's favor. For all he knows this Whitey guy's another Leon. Part of some reckless scheme that'll backfire with worse results. Hal's secret "business." Mrs. B's loathing of him. They're clear signs Paul needs to heed.

"Let it go," he tells himself, repeating Dr. Fabiani's mantra for any thoughts that can lead to obsession.

Whitey shuffles over to the table. He clears up as if no one's there.

CHAPTER 12

MAX RUBS HIS aching shoulder with some liniment. "Frigging slut. Goddamn baby factory."

"Could you change that record please?" Paul says.

"It's her fault my bursitis is acting up."

"And I still have a pastel drawing to do."

"A drawing," his father says as if it shouldn't count as homework. "Then move smarter to work faster. I keep telling you. Use your scraper like this."

"That way hurts."

"Not if you angle it right."

Paul could do a better job if he used his drawing hand. But he doesn't want to make it sore as he did on Saturday when he worked alone. He watches Max give another demonstration. "You should make a training film."

"Don't get wise. We got a long day together."

And they do. Since early morning father and son have scraped the kitchen walls in the family flat. It's their third Sunday working on the project. Stubborn patches of old wallpaper defy removal. Without a sculptor's care the aging, fragile plaster beneath can crumble; leave huge holes to screen, spackle and size, with drying time needed for layered applications. Four such mishaps occurred the first day. All of them Paul's fault. Max was furious. Now he wants all the scraping finished by dinner. The wallpapering will have to wait for another weekend.

Only a month after the new renter, a single mother, moved upstairs, one of her six kids—the four-year-old—christened the flat with a sink overflow. The runoff seeped into the kitchen below. Some plaster buckled. Layers of sodden wallpaper curled like gift ribbon. The damage was isolated to one wall, but the entire room needed repapering.

Max pops open his third beer of the day. "Frigging slut," he starts up again.

"Blame your good buddy down the club," Paul says. "If Rube wasn't seeing her on the sly she wouldn't be living here. You should make him scrape the walls."

"Your mother's got a big mouth. Where is she anyway? How long's it take to pick out wallpaper when she says she doesn't give a damn?" He wrings his sponge dry over the large bucket. "This water's gone cold again."

Paul takes his cue. He empties the heavy bucket into the toilet, refills it in the bathroom tub with water hot as he can stand. He measures in vinegar to get a twenty-percent solution. The peeling mixture makes old wallpaper smell like sauerkraut. But the stuff works. On his return, he nearly trips over an extension cord snaked across the floor. It's plugged into another room to power the work lamp and the refrigerator. Electricity in the kitchen's turned off as a precaution. Focused on rough walls, the work light casts the dark room in dramatic shadows. It's as if he and his father were mining for treasure.

Which gives him an idea. "Maybe I'll do a take on the paintings at Lascaux."

"La where?"

"For my homework. I could do a parody of the prehistoric cave paintings. They're near a small French town. It's called Lascaux. The walls have hunting scenes with huge animals. Tiny men with spears. They're famous."

"I never heard of them."

Paul stifles a comeback. "I can copy a hunting scene from my survey book. Make it a mural over a sink, like it's in a modern-day caveman kitchen. Then I'll draw a Neanderthal dressed in an apron. He's sliding a plate into a dish rack with his big, hairy hand. It'd be funny, don't you think?"

"Not really. But it only matters what your teacher thinks."

"Oh, he'll like it well enough. And while I'm talking about living like a caveman, can we put my bedroom door back up while we're doing all this home improvement? It's been four years. A kid my age should have some privacy. Dr. Fabiani said so."

"That door came down because you needed to see that guy. It'll stay that way until you don't."

"Thanks for the vote of confidence."

"You're welcome." Max stands back from his work to gauge their progress.

Paul joins him if only for a break. Everywhere islands of obstinate wallpaper mark the rough plaster surface. They create a splotchy, multi-colored effect. Bold, florid patterns from early layers seem to float near busy, geometric designs applied years later. They form a partial history of the occupants' taste over many decades. The wall appears haggard, spent. He wouldn't be surprised if it collapsed into powder like a mummified corpse. He turns to his father. In the chiaroscuro Max seems much like the plaster. He tries again to connect with the man. "You know Leonardo Da Vinci? The artist who painted the *Mona Lisa*? He said that—"

"Mona Lisa, Mona Lisa, men have named you," Max sings. And he's off with a sluggish rendition of the pop ballad, including a lengthy scat of the instrumental bit in the middle. He still has a solid baritone despite his chain smoking and beer drinking. Not to mention the toxic dust he inhales at the factory. And the shouting matches with his wife that leave him hoarse for days.

Before Max started crooning, Paul wanted to tell his father about Da Vinci's advice to young painters. He read about it for school. How Leonardo said to study old walls that are stained, have different colored stones in them. How—by looking hard enough—an artist can envision any resemblance. See every kind of landscape or person. Absolutely anything that exists in the real world. He thought the old master's counsel might ease their task. He and Max

177

could share impressions while they work. Make a joke of it. What a dumb idea. He sees that now. His father would only scorn the suggestion; view it as more useless stuff taught by a weirdo school.

He marinates some more wallpaper scraps with hot vinegar solution and waits for it to work. He uses the time—and Max's musical interlude—to apply Leonardo's advice. At first the paper islands he stares at throb against a gray plaster sea. But it doesn't take long for him to detect Hal's profile in a sharply outlined patch, one with geometric shapes that run helter-skelter along the surface. Another patch, a hot red floral one, recalls the man in the park. The man who chased him. The man his parents didn't want to hear about when he tried to tell them at dinner that night. Their silence left him wondering if they were disappointed with the outcome or merely indifferent.

"Are you warm, are you real, Mona Lisa," Max finishes, "Or just a cold and lonely, lovely work of art."

"That was nice," Paul says.

"Nice?"

"Good as a pro." He resents having to overpraise his father, who refuses to say anything positive about his artwork.

Max still seems disappointed. He scratches his swelling belly, turns on the portable radio. "I'm taking this to the factory tomorrow. The one down there's shot."

"Fine with me." The set belongs to Paul, a birthday gift

of several years ago he doesn't use. "I got the AC attachment for it somewhere."

"So when can I tell Otto you'll be starting work?"

"Think I saw that attachment in my room. I'll go look."

"Look later."

Paul shrugs and checks a sodden patch with his scraper.

"So—when?" Max says.

"What?"

"I been waiting a week now. Otto needs an answer."

The answer Paul dreads giving. He had a little speech prepared, very diplomatic, for when the time came. Now he can't remember. "About this summer."

"You don't want to start right away. Is that it?"

"Not exactly."

"Then what exactly?"

"I won't be able to start at all." Paul turns from his father. He scrapes hard at a stubborn patch.

"Quit that," Max says. "You'll break the goddamn plaster again." He commandeers the tool. "Get your butt off that ladder." He grunts at the slow descent, shakes another cigarette from his pack and lights it, adding to smoke clouds already fouling the room. "Now I want an answer. No bullshit. No hemming and hawing." He waits as long as it takes to open another beer. "What're you, off in outer space again? You need a frigging countdown to make a landing?"

"I made other plans," Paul says.

179

"Other plans?"

"For the entire summer."

Max whistles in mock admiration. "Mr. Big Shot over here's got other plans."

"To go to school," Paul says. "They have a special arts program for juniors and seniors. It's two months long," he adds, although it's only six weeks. "If I do well enough, I can earn some extra credit and boost my grades." But most of all the classes will keep him safe. Keep him from the sweatshop that routinely flouts child labor law and most safety regulations, and makes him work long hours on dangerous machinery. Last summer he almost crushed his left hand. The summer before that, his right.

Max guzzles down his beer. He starts to pace, mumbles to himself, working his way to a hot and lingering burn. His son knows the pattern well.

"You tell your mother about this?"

"Nope."

"What about your shrink?"

Paul doesn't answer. Max often complains that Dr. Fabiani conspires against him at every turn.

"You like seeing that man every week?"

"You know I do."

"He don't come cheap. I know that even more."

"The state pays for most of him," Paul says. "He told me so himself."

"Maybe he only wants you to feel good. If he's so damn

180

cheap, why do I work o.t. at the factory? Why do I deliver meat every Saturday?"

"But you keep the extra money you make. You spend it down the club."

"Your mother's full of shit."

"She didn't tell me. You did."

"Now I know you're in outer space again."

"No I'm not. It was last year. You were feeling pretty good after a night downstairs. I heard you and Mom go at it. She wanted that money for the house kitty. You said no. That it was all yours to spend on yourself."

Max glowers. His brindled cheeks get puffy. "You were eavesdropping."

"It's hard not to when I don't have a bedroom door."

"Don't start on that again. You heard wrong because you were snooping. But I'll tell you one thing you didn't hear. That money you make during summer helps a lot. Take a look at this place. You think your old man's rich? Got money to burn? How about I work every day of the week to pay for that voodoo crank?" He wags his finger close to his son's face. "I know what your problem is. You got it easy all your life. You never worked hard to survive, like in the Depression when we . . ."

Paul tunes out the history lesson. He knows, by heart, the saga recounted on that subject whenever there's a discussion about money. Somewhere during the monologue, his inattention must show. Max stops midstream. He sputters. A minor tremor runs along his body. Paul stares at his father's nose. Last year Max had a close call. If his nose hadn't bled, he might've suffered a stroke. The doctor said. Paul isn't sure where the pills are kept. He has no idea how fast they might work. Max never takes them because he'd have to stop drinking.

"You okay, Dad?"

"No, I'm not okay. And you want to know why? I'll tell you why. You got no respect for hard work, that's why. And I mean real work. You think making art's work? You think you can earn a living at it? You don't know a damn thing. A kid like you with your head in the clouds, you need to be shown. It's the only way. I'll have to draw *you* a picture this time."

"Of what?"

"How I'll spend my Sundays if you don't go down the factory."

Paul can hear his father rummage through the front bedroom closet, digging for something. He stays in the kitchen, not caring to look. A moment ago he wanted his imagination to run free; now he works hard to stifle it, not connect sounds to objects.

"Come over here." Max stands at the front door in the parlor. He carries a beat-up wooden box covered in earth-colored stains. The kind that might've inspired Leonardo. Built of unfinished pine, the box appears homemade. It has short, fat legs with an opening on each side. There's a peculiar handle on top. Paul doesn't recognize its shape until he's up close. His father gives him two small bottles. "Fill these up with water."

"Why?"

"Because they're half empty. And make sure you screw the caps on tight."

Paul doesn't move. He wants to refuse, but his father still has that tremor. Is the cause simple anger or something else? He looks hard at Max's nose, the bloodshot eyes. He heard somewhere that pupils grow large during a stroke. Or did he read it in a story?

"What the hell are you gawking at?"

"Nothing."

"Then quit your stalling."

Paul does as he's told. He watches Max slide the filled bottles into the box through a side opening. "Where we going with that thing?"

"You'll find out."

Tremor or no, Paul wants to hold his ground about school. "I already signed up, you know. It's a done deal."

"So was you working at the factory."

"Yeah, but—"

"No more buts." Max swings open the door. "You first, Mr. Big Shot."

Outside Paul's building the street is crowded with club members—or hyenas as he often thinks of them, especially late at night when their carousing disturbs his sleep, and early on weekends when they blast the jukebox and sing along. The men are out enjoying a balmy afternoon. Some sit on the long bench underneath a picture window. Others lean against cars or clog the gray sidewalk in islands of three or four. Most are Max's age and older. The youngest are the first to greet him; the first to notice the box he holds. They watch father and son make a beeline for the club door, left open to the fine air.

Inside more men line the well-stocked, mirrored bar. Others hover around tables packed with card players. The juke box wails. Raised voices echo along the brown tin ceiling, along dusty walls laced with old mirrors that feature stenciled liquor ads. The din shocks the ears. Paul's anyway. Even the men's reflections seem to be yelling. Meanwhile the cigar stench nearly overwhelms. The place becomes another smoky cave, this one provoking dread instead of inspiration. A cave filled with men he despises. Men who regard him with subtle scorn. And some with veiled desire. Men who'll shame him and his father in the name of friendship.

"Hey Maxie-boy!" Rube's grating voice soars above the clamor. "And look who you brought with you." He eyes the box with keen interest. It would be this tall, burly showoff to get things rolling. He and his cronies form a curious huddle around the arrivals. Like Max, they seem older than their years, flabby and bitter. Paul knows them only by their nicknames.

"What's up with the box?" Peanuts says.

Blacky nudges it with his foot. "Ain't seen a kit like that in years."

"It's from back in the day," Max tells them, "when we shined shoes."

"I never shined shoes," Nightwalker says.

"No," Rube says, "you just stole what you needed."

"Listen to sticky fingers over here."

"Who you calling sticky fingers?"

"KP's right," says Johnny the Polack. "I remember you got me in trouble all the time."

"You got yourself in trouble. You were too damn slow on the getaway."

"It was on account of my flat feet."

"More like your fat ass," Bones says to explosive laughter. He waddles in a circle like a knock-kneed duck.

"Talk about a big butt." Gaby whacks his friend there, and a playful wrestling match begins. The spectacle attracts more onlookers. Some call out bets on who'll win. The two men bump their way past juke-box fanatics and card players. They tumble back into the kitchen on a zigzag course to the reception hall, where they quit from exhaustion, splayed across some chairs that line the dreary, wood-paneled room. The shouting crowd that followed them retreats in disappointment. Rube and his cronies remain. So do father and son, swept up by the fast-moving ruckus. Paul was squeezed against Max the whole time. The shoe-shine box kept bumping against his leg, a constant reminder of his mortification, and his decision to remain firm, not surrender the coming summer to despair and potential hazard.

His father sets up shop fast, humming a manic tune from the swing era. He lays the box near a tall bar chair left over from a party. He trots into the kitchen for a foot stool, places it before his customers' high throne. His knees crack as he squats on the stool. His stomach sinks low between his thighs. Paul can't look anymore. Nor can he face the other men. His father opens the box. Still humming he arranges his gear in order of use on the blue linoleum floor.

"What's this about, Maxie?" Rube says.

"You got money problems?" KP asks.

"What I got's a kid who don't want to help carry his own weight. A kid who don't want a good summer job his old man kissed ass to get him. Now I got to teach him a lesson. Show him the value of work—*any* kind of work— so he'll do the right thing." He stops there. Everyone turns to Paul, expectant. He ignores the men, has no intention of giving his side about school. Why should he? What business is it of theirs? Who are they to judge one way or the other?

Max waves a dismissive hand. "See what I mean? It's like you're talking to a wall." He whips a snap rag against the box's metal foot rest. "So who's first? Who wants a shine the good old-fashioned way?"

The men eye each other. Most of them seem embarrassed. Blacky turns to Peanuts. Johnny the Polack shakes his head and elbows Nightwalker. KP defers to Gaby who passes to Bones who nudges Rube who finally says, "You charge old-fashioned prices for an old-fashioned shine?"

"Go screw yourself," Max tells him.

Everyone laughs but Paul. A fee is reached after some haggling. Rube sets his burly form on the tall, narrow stool. He squints behind thick glasses to avoid heavy smoke from his stogy. With a hairy, jeweled hand he rolls the cigar in his mouth.

And the shoe-shine boy gets to work. He grabs one of the bottles Paul filled with water. It holds diluted cleaning fluid meant for brown leather only.

Nightwalker drapes an arm around Johnny the Polack, who's busy rubbing his eyes with a handkerchief. "Take a look at this crybaby over here."

"What's the matter with you?" Blacky says.

"I'm feeling all nostalgic. The times we used to have."

"He gets the same way when he loses at cards," KP says.

But the mood is catching. "I miss the old days too," Peanuts says. "Ain't that why we come here?"

"You come to get away from your wife," Rube tells him.

"Look who's talking." Gaby rolls his eyes up to the ceiling and makes a crude gesture.

"Sounds to me like someone's jealous."

"Do you bang her in front of all her kids, or do you take her down here when the place's closed?"

"Watch your mouth guys." Max nods at his son.

"You're awful bossy for a bootblack."

Rube's joke falls flat. Max dips his head lower. He rubs the leather hard with a little round brush.

"What's that you're humming now?" KP asks him.

"Heart of My Heart."

Gaby starts on the lyrics. Max and the others join in. They sing about a gang of rough and ready teenagers. Kids who liked to hang out on a street corner harmonizing. Kids turned into gloomy men who regret having to part for good, presumably to grow up.

Paul listens to the sappy refrain. He knows the words too, having heard them slurred—year in, year out—through his bedroom floor many times. Often the song played in his mind for days. It haunted him. Meanwhile Max seems strangely content. No sign of a tremor now. Paul imagines his father going backwards in time, getting smaller, and trying to take his son with him. The man becomes a boy again. A happy bootblack shrinking down to the size of a baby, down to something so small and mindless it could fit in a shoe-shine box.

CHAPTER 13

EVEN ON GREENWICH Avenue Paul can smell kerosene from his nine-hour day at the factory. His nose feels stuffed with grinding dust. His lips taste metallic. He should wear a breathing mask at work. And serious ear protectors. But he doesn't know better. No one there including his father uses them. All summer long the factory stench and the sound of grinding metal give him hallucinatory dreams, as if he were under ether. He awakens with his heart thumping, his ears buzzing.

Stubborn grit clogs his fingernails and knuckles, the deeper lines of his palms. He pockets his hands so they won't show. A long-sleeved shirt hides more stains washing can't remove. His dark-blond bangs curl in the heat and humidity. They dangle above blue eyes itchy from fatigue and factory pollution. He walks the busy Greenwich Village streets longing for something to happen, for someone attractive and pleasant and safe to want him. At times he'd be grateful for an hour with a decent enough taker. He's had several such encounters. They left him disappointed, feeling politely discarded afterwards. He dreams of meeting a smart, sophisticated guy. A mature, established man who'd take a lasting interest in him, teach him how to live his life, remold him from scratch.

He checks out the pedestrian traffic. But he's too shy. And he walks too fast for a kid on the make. It's the only way he's figured to avoid strangers he'd rather not meet. Suspicious guys, hungry guys who pounce at the slightest eye contact, can't take a courteous no for an answer. They can squander his precious free time. The tall street clock on Eighth Avenue reads eleven. He has work early tomorrow. At least it's only a half day, a Saturday.

Fatigue hits him. He needs to conserve his energy for the slog home. He's ready to call it a night when he hears a car horn blast from across the broad avenue. Tires screech. A big blue car makes a reckless U-turn. It idles near him, the engine growling. Tinted windows obscure the inside.

Jerry tumbles out the front passenger door. The wild-haired carrot top looks good in his guinea tee, his tight black jeans that coat shapely legs. Drugged-out hazel eyes squint from his porcelain face. The two boys met in Dr. Fabiani's waiting room. It was Jerry who told Paul about the Village scene, accompanied him on his first few trips, since he still has trouble negotiating directions alone.

"What you up too, hot stuff?"

"Just hanging out," Paul says.

"I'm on a date." Jerry thumbs at the driver's side and pants in delight. "Want a ride back to Jersey?"

Paul shrugs. He's met Jerry's "dates" before. All of them were downer druggies he wouldn't trust behind the wheel. He squats low to check out the driver and almost

190

falls backwards, amazed to see Hal sitting there. He never would've guessed the two boys... Not even for a night. Then again, why would he? He waits for Hal to let on that they know each other. But it doesn't happen. He plays along and introduces himself.

"Looks kind of crowded in there," he says.

"You can sit between us. There's plenty room." The girl in the back seat talks like a breathy debutante or a Miss Universe contestant. She has a Spanish accent, wears a lot of makeup. Her beehive hairdo almost touches the car roof. Only she's not a girl, Paul sees, on closer inspection. "My name's Alice." The bony young guy pats his flat chest, covered in a spangled pink halter. "And this is Mia."

"Nice to meet you both."

The other guy, a tall, broad-featured brunette, could be Alice's brother—or sister. They both look mixed-race Puerto Rican.

"So get in already." Hal's mischievous smile lingers in brown eyes that seem more lushly fringed than ever. In the rearview mirror he regards his new passenger. Paul smiles back to be polite. And because, despite their last encounter, despite knowing all he knows about the boy, and all he doesn't know, he can't help liking what he sees.

"Let me out right here," Jerry says, "or I'll jump out."

Hal slams the breaks on Ferry Street in the Ironbound section of Newark, not far from Penn Station.

Jerry checks out the deserted commercial avenue. He's several long blocks from his home.

"What's with the bitch routine?" Hal says.

"Not for nothing, but I thought we had a date. Now all of a sudden you want to drop *me* off first?"

Hal doesn't answer. Everyone in the car knows why. Alice and Mia flutter their false eyelashes at Paul. Hal's paid attention mostly to him since the drive began, making small talk, cracking jokes, still pretending for whatever reason, or no reason at all, that they're strangers. Paul wants to walk Jerry home, but can't offer. He'd have a long trek back to the North Ward. It's past twelve already. And the car seat's so comfortable. If not for Hal's lavish attention, he'd have nodded off. "I'll call you when I get home," he says.

"Don't fucking bother." Jerry slides out the car. He slams the door, almost trips over his own feet. Chin raised high, he snaps his fingers at the driver and everyone else. He weaves down the empty street swearing nonstop.

Paul stares at the thick red globs splattered along a floor so worn it resembles tree bark. The small television's on, broadcasting nothing but snow. A weak, ghostly voice emanates from the tinny speaker. He backs out of the first-floor apartment into the dark hallway, ready to sprint down the street, bad neighborhood or no. Mia and Alice confer in Spanish. They talk fast. Too fast for Paul to follow, despite his three years of high school classes.

"It's only ketchup," Mia announces.

"No kidding," Hal says. "Real blood doesn't look like that."

Alice checks out a small puddle close up to make sure. She seems embarrassed. But Mia's all smiles. "My husband Calvin did this. We had a fight about me going out. He's so possessive." She hugs herself, shakes her head indulgently. "Sometimes he gets melodramatical when he . . ." She makes a fluttery drinking motion near her wide, painted mouth. "I must go to him." She trots in her purple espadrilles down a short hallway to a closed door. Her charm bracelets tinkle like small bells.

"Calvin's from West Virginia," Alice says, like it explains the guy's behavior. "He works in the plating factory down Neck. Part-time. With me and Mia. We share this place together. We share everything, even hair shampoo." Mia's sobs penetrate the closed door. A strange, deep voice joins in, rumbling in a thick Appalachian accent baffling to Paul as rapid-fire Spanish. "Maybe we should leave." He's surprised Hal hasn't made a move already.

"Don't," Alice says. "They're only going to make up. Let's go in the kitchen, away from all this." She tip-toes around the ketchup slicks that dot the floor.

Paul follows her steps. Not until he sits at the orange metal table does he notice the walls and floor have patterns that move. Cockroaches wander everywhere. Unfazed by people or the sudden light, they appear well-fed and lazy.

And they come in different types. Some have long bodies with huge wings. Others are compact and shiny. Paul's never seen roaches in a person's home before, only in some New York diner. That dive had an army of the insects. They seemed to explode from decorative wine bottles hanging from the ceiling. He left without eating. Or paying. Now he looks for a signal to split. But the other boy sits beside him as if everything's normal. Hal's grown even more muscular and adult looking since the spring. He fills out his guinea tee and jeans to bursting. His pale-olive skin glistens in the stifling room. Despite the hour he seems a little wired.

Alice opens the refrigerator. Hinges creak. Some of the roaches tramping along the door scatter. They make for the table. Paul taps his feet hard to scare them off. "May I get you some ice water or beer?" Alice sounds prim and proper, as if a bug army isn't on dawn patrol around her. "And I see we have orange juice!"

Paul declines. Hal doesn't bother answering. He swallows so hard it's audible. His Adam's apple slides up and down his throat like a smooth walnut. "Why don't you leave us alone a while, Alice?"

"Why don't you leave us alone a while," she echoes sadly and slinks into the parlor.

"That was nice," Paul says.

"Don't worry about Alice. We got an agreement, a business arrangement."

Paul doesn't ask what kind. He remembers the rude way Hal treated Whitey at the luncheonette. Those two have a business arrangement as well. He's not sure how to read the other boy's gaze. "How've you been?"

Hal just keeps looking.

Paul tries again. "Enjoying summer vacation?"

"Been working at Overbrook since school got out."

"What's that?"

"A big loony bin up in Cedar Grove. I'm an orderly there. I keep the nut jobs in order." He flexes his thick arm, pulls up his guinea tee, showing off a smooth, muscle-plated chest, which he scratches. The pink marks slowly fade. "Mostly I work the building sectioned to the criminally insane. Got the job through a friend there."

"They let a high school kid do that?"

"I'm supposed to be working with small kids and old people. That's what my bullshit paperwork says anyway. Had to show the clown who hired me I could handle myself. We got into a wrestling match right in his office. The closet case thinks he's a tough guy. I had him huffing and puffing in no time. But he was really enjoying himself, know what I mean? It was hard to keep a straight face. Half the people who work there ought to be committed if you ask me."

"Sounds like a scary job."

"Nothing I can't handle."

"I wouldn't want to work there."

"They'd have your ass for dinner." Hal breaks out in loud laughter.

"It's not that funny."

"Not you. I took Jerry there once."

"Jerry? You're laughing about Jerry?"

Hal cracks up again.

Paul feels bad about the way he left things. He should've walked the kid home. It'd be better than sitting in this roach-infested kitchen. He slides his chair around to keep the vermin at bay.

Still laughing, his cheeks wet with tears, Hal makes for the refrigerator. He takes the orange juice Alice offered earlier. The half-gallon carton's brand new. Its front panel has a cartoon of a scantily clad, brown-skinned woman. She has a pile of fruit on her head. He points to the image and smirks. "Reminds me of Alice." He squeezes the top open and offers it.

Paul shakes his head. He won't put a glass to his mouth. Not from this kitchen. He changes his mind after Hal guzzles straight from the carton's pristine spout. "I'll have some." He reaches out.

"Come and get it."

Paul walks unsteadily, his legs numb from the hard chair, the tension of keeping vile insects at bay. He drinks greedily. The cold, acidic juice eases his parched throat. "Tell me about Jerry and this Overbrook place."

"One night I took the kid up there on a little tour. Kept my regular ward for last. Once I get Jerry in the rec area, where the inmates can hang out if they're manageable, I tell him the room's full of murderers and rapists. He starts looking around all bug-eyed. That's when I disappear. Pretend to leave him there. All the time I'm in the hallway at the entrance door, watching through the grate." He cracks up again, leans his hot, wet head against Paul until he can continue. "So the kid's having a fit. I can see he's got the shakes gawking at those drugged-out zombies. One of them lets out a scream for no reason. Like some wild animal. Jerry looks about to scream too. I let him hang a little more. Then I waltz back in like everything's normal, before he has a fit or something."

"That's a crappy thing to do," Paul says. "Especially to a nervous kid like Jerry."

He's not sure he was heard. Hal's bent over, doubled up with laughter. He clears his throat and spits in the sink, rinses his mouth with juice. "It was a joke, man. A harmless joke. Nothing would've happened to him. There were two orderlies in the room the whole time. Jerry could've noticed."

"Yeah, but that would've spoiled your fun."

"Stop being such a tight ass."

"Then stop being a creep."

"If I'm a creep, what was the kid doing with me tonight?"

197

"And where is he now, Mr. Nice Guy?"

"Whose fault is that?"

Paul doesn't answer, knowing he shares blame for Jerry's latest upset. He tucks his shirt in his pants, checks for his wallet, his house key. "I have to go. Got an early day—like I told you twice in the car before you went and stopped here anyway."

"Come on. Stay a little longer." Hal gently nudges Paul against the refrigerator door, his hands roaming. "We can use Alice's room."

"You got to be kidding." Paul jerks free. All he can think of is cockroaches getting on his body, inside his clothes, hitching a ride home, where they set up housekeeping.

Hal's face grows tense, mean looking, the angular symmetry distorted. His eyes squint like he's staring at the sun. His right arm crosses his chest, poised to deliver a smack.

Paul doesn't flinch or try to protect himself.

There's a stare-off.

Hal lowers his hand, slides it in his back pocket. The tension seems to drain from his face. His shoulders slump. He looks down at his tan work boots. "I'll take you home."

"No thanks. I feel like walking." This must sound like bullshit. Who'd want to walk alone at this hour, in this neighborhood? But now that he said it, Paul can't take it back.

"Sure you want to do that? I won't pull anything, even

though you sent me signals all during the ride. Getting dreamy eyed. Cruising me in the rearview mirror every time I looked. In fact, go screw yourself. Take a walk for all I care. I wouldn't drive you across the frigging street."

Paul wishes he could start over and get asked again. But the offer doesn't happen. He walks into the parlor, past Alice, spread out on the sofa where she badly feigns sleep. He negotiates the ketchup puddles gone brown, smelling putrid.

The empty thoroughfare looks awfully scary in the black, humid night. Every third step he wants to glance behind him, but refrains. He puts a lot of space between himself and the old cemetery he passes. It's the same, fenced-in graveyard where he and Max repaired the flat tire years ago. Only now he's on the yard's opposite side. The side that borders this tough area filled with dilapidated row houses. Their windows and doors evoke grim, forbidding expressions. With every step he hears grumbling noises. Or thinks he does. If he weren't so tired he'd sprint. Behind him the grumbling gets louder, sounds angrier. He quickens his pace, but with care. His gait's wobbly from fatigue.

"Hey, Paulie," he hears beside him.

"You scared the hell out of me."

"Yeah, well." Hal grins like it couldn't be helped. His beautiful head hangs out the passenger seat. "Cut the shit and get in. Something happens to you, I'd feel like it's my fault."

"That'd be a welcome change," Paul says and they both laugh. But in the car they stay quiet, ride in silence. Hal parks in front of the men's club. It's closed for the night. The yellow lamps that frame the door cast a welcoming glow. Paul listens to the other boy's breathing, smells his sweat, vaguely reminiscent of clove or nutmeg. "Thanks," he says.

Hal stares ahead, his jaw slack, like he's in a trance, or about to doze off.

Paul grabs the door handle.

"I'm thinking of joining the Army maybe," Hal says. "Soon as I graduate next year."

"Why'd you want to do that?"

"A guy from my group home signed up a while back. He stopped by for a visit his first leave. Said enlisting was the best move he ever made. Told me all the things he's been doing and learning. So I'm thinking, why not join and get a leg up? I'll probably get drafted anyway since I sure won't be going to college."

"What about your other stuff?"

"What other stuff?"

"Your business. Can't you do something with that?"

"It ain't consistent. Know what I mean?"

"How'd I know since you never told me what it is?"

"My friend at Overbrook," Hal says. "The guy who helped me get the orderly job. Sometimes he has access to the pharmacy. He lifts stuff whenever he can. Just enough not to get caught or trigger a special inventory check. Uppers, downers, painkillers—whatever he can cop. He passes them to me. I sell them to pill heads like Whitey and Alice and Jerry." He pats the dashboard, strokes it as if it were a pet. "That's how I got my wheels. But it's nowhere near a living. And there's always a risk. I can't get put away again. Not as an adult. That's doing a whole different kind of time."

"The Coast Guard's better," Paul says.

"Than jail? Hell yeah."

"If you enlist. The Coast Guard's better than the Army."

"How'd you know?"

"You'll be safer on a ship over here than in some jungle in Vietnam. That's probably where you'd wind up in the Army. Your friend too."

"I ain't scared."

"You ought to be. The butcher's son who lives up the street, he lost an arm three weeks into his tour of duty. He used to be a nice guy. Now he's nothing but mean. He gets drunk a lot, always looking for fights. You're enough of a prick as it is. So if you have to go somewhere—which you don't—you should go Coast Guard." Paul doesn't look, but he's certain Hal's smiling at him. The car gets even warmer.

"I'll check it out then, maybe."

"You do that."

"What about you? Got plans?"

"It won't be the service. Any kind of service. College I guess—if I can get in one and find a way to pay for it. I'm not exactly the best student in the world."

"You could get drafted if you don't."

"That won't happen."

"You sound real sure."

"I am. My shrink said he'd take care of it. Said he'd write a letter for the Board if he had to. No way they'd want me after that."

"What'll it say?"

"What do you think?"

"Shit," Hal says. "That's almost like having a criminal record. Maybe worse."

"Not everyone's an idiot."

"Oh yeah?"

"I'm not talking about you. I mean people in general. Smart people like my teachers, and people I've met in New York. They seem to manage really well."

"I know some older guys," Hal says. "They got 86ed from their jobs after they got found out."

"What's that mean?"

"They got canned is what it means. They were smart guys too. Worked for smart people in smart offices. Now they got crap jobs or none at all."

Paul can't think what to say. And what difference would words make? It's way too late for this kind of talk. He'll be walking in his sleep at work if he doesn't get enough shut-eye. He digs in his pocket for the house key. It'd be easier to get it outside the car, but that's not where he wants to be. Hal reaches over, stays his hand. Paul gives in. He sinks into the thick seat, closes his eyes for what seems only a minute. He dreams he's floating in darkness. A hand rubs the nape of his neck, squeezing muscles, massaging. "Oh that's good. Just kill me now."

"Not yet," he hears, close to his ear. So close it tickles.

He opens his eyes, surprised to see a brick factory in the darkness. Water churns. He can smell its polluted flow. "Where are we?"

"Drove us along the tracks," Hal says, "between the stream and the factories. No one'll see us here. Let's get in back."

"I'm beat. Help me crawl over." Grabbed by the waist, Paul's boosted over the front. He stretches out on the cool black leather, one foot on the floor, an arm draped overhead. He grabs hold of the window crank.

Hal gets out. He opens the back door and makes a place for himself on top the other boy. Paul feels his belt getting unbuckled. He arches his back to help. His pants slide past his knees. Seat leather sticks to bare pale skin. Large hands roam him. A warm mouth travels everywhere, settles on an unexpected place. Is this a dream? Is he dreaming? He gazes at the car roof's black interior, his starless sky. He steadies his breath, waits for pleasure to overtake him.

But the stream's reeking flow interferes. It reminds him

of gritty water pumped through grinding machines all day. He tries to expel the job from his head, from his dream with Hal. But it's too late. The buzz and grind and screech of the factory commandeer his ears. He smells kerosene, oily sawdust. He's no longer in the car, but lying beside Hal on the wide lunch table at work, its surface etched with graffiti. Machines shriek and hiss at them under glaring florescent lights. Steel dust mists the air. But there are no workers. They're alone. Outside the car window Paul sees the same ugly bushes, the same homely Sumac trees that grow all along the tracks, far as the eye can see, as if looking into his future.

Heat in the factory builds. Heat from the machines, and two young bodies gliding against each other. Warmth melds them together. Their sweat mixes with factory odors. Everything moves faster, faster still. The machinery hum turns into a growl. It comes from Hal, his mouth pressed against Paul's ear.

Their breathing calms, steadies. The smell of steel and rancid oil dissipates, replaced by that of warm leather, wet bodies drying. Gone too are the rumbling factory noises. Everything falls silent, except the stream. In the quiet Paul dreams that he and Hal rest on nothing but air. Pure, fresh air. He's aware from some watchful part of his mind that this calm won't last, that the two will separate, the daily misery return. And then he dreams he doesn't care.

CHAPTER 14

SOMETHING NEW APPEARS with every approach. Revelers have a spectral quality as they emerge from the dark and weedy lot used for parking. Two rosy-cheeked women dressed as doughboys walk arm-in-arm. They're followed by a Roman senator in a lamé toga. A pink mermaid sports an iridescent tailfin and a brassiere made of shells. A buccaneer and Russian Cossack materialize from the shadows. The Cossack's red beard flows to his knees. On yet another go around the block, Paul sees a troupe of guys in drag leave a station wagon that resembles a hearse. Their outfits range from winged angel to leather-clad hooker. Some burly men in suits show up during a later pass, all of them stone-faced.

He waits for a lull in the foot traffic before making his sixth foray. From a distance he peers into the bar's smoky windows. Many patrons have come and gone each time he slowly circled the block while feigning disinterest, ignoring the occasional whistle from a drunken merrymaker. He's not walked this old strip of downtown Newark before. Its grimy industrial buildings, no higher than four stories, must've gone up during the prior century. The later part anyway. They have a doleful cast, as if mourning what used to fill the empty lots that lead to the Passaic River, where water reflects city lights.

He has a mind not to show. Why should he? Not a word from Hal since their summer encounter. Then yesterday, right after school, he gets a brief, impersonal phone call ending with an offhanded invitation and a guarantee of safe entry. And he's supposed to jump? Disappear from the flat and his doorless bedroom late at night?

He rallies enough nerve for a closer look.

A cab pulls up. The tiny Samurai who jumps out strikes a militant pose, waves an enormous fake sword that wiggles in its handle.

"Sayonara baby!" He aims the prop at Paul.

"Quit showing off and get me out," someone says from the cab.

The Samurai gives Paul his mock blade to hold. He helps dislodge the hefty passenger who's dressed as a nurse. The guy's makeup appears spackled on. His wig and nurse's cap hit the doorframe and come askew. He squints at Paul. "Aren't you something. The only costume you need is your birthday suit."

"I saw him first," the Samurai says.

"You've been saying that all night."

"Wear your glasses then."

"These don't fit my frames." The nurse flutters his long false lashes. They resemble fans; heavy, spidery fans that seem to have a life of their own.

"You coming from a Halloween party?" Paul asks.

"Goldie's," the Samurai says.

"Don't know her."

"It's a bar, baby, not a home." The nurse clutches his chest. "Be still my foolish heart."

"It better be," the Samurai says. "I smell jailbait."

"When'd that ever stop you? Meanwhile I'm Martin, and this pint-sized warrior's Charlie."

Paul introduces himself. He listens to more flattering repartee and trails the duo inside. He uses Martin's wide frame as cover. He still can pull a 180 without being spotted if he finds the atmosphere too intimidating or the promise of safe entry false. It'd serve Hal right for—

"You old fuck-face," Charlie shouts.

He and Martin peel off to the left side of the long wooden bar. They air kiss someone who's lathered in ghoulish makeup and wearing a purple vampire outfit. He's with a brawny Peter Pan, a bearded Tinker Bell complete with blinking wand, and a female bride of Frankenstein whose soaring fright wig sparkles with glitter.

Paul doesn't follow the amiable pair. He wants to avoid an intro although they seem to have forgotten him anyway. He falls in with the chaotic flow, steering clear of the bar. Passersby jostle him. They're dressed in costume or not, drunk or not. On the make or not. This must be the year for sequins. Every other guy in drag wears a dress plastered with the stuff. Pinks, blues and greens dazzle his eyes. A

207

squad of pretty young women in cheerleader outfits wave pom-poms in his face as they pass. The crush makes him lightheaded. Maybe it's a sign to leave. He spots Hal at a table in the back. He gets close enough to make angry eye contact before reversing course. A familiar large hand reaches out to him from behind a tall black woman in a zoot suit.

"You were supposed to meet me outside," he says.

"And you were supposed to show an hour ago."

"I did, you unreliable prick."

"Guess I'm the bad boy." Hal extends his palms for smacking and draws back when the offer's accepted. He looks finer than fine. The mellow lighting gives his handsome face a golden glow like in a Rembrandt portrait. His short leather jacket has a tight fit.

Paul feels the soft material. "Hope you didn't steal this one."

"No costume?" Hal says.

"Where's yours?"

"That's for mugs."

"Like some of the people you're with?"

"What people?"

Paul cranes his neck to view the table, abandoned now except for empty glasses.

"Everyone's circulating," Hal says. "Let's go upstairs before a bartender IDs you."

"You said there wouldn't be any problem."

"There won't if you hang upstairs."

"What about waiters?"

"Ain't none. Only some busboy runs up and down to clear tables. Guy can barely speak American."

"Then all my worries are over."

"I knew you'd be a pain." Hal fingers through his wallet, hands Paul a duplicate driver's license with some stranger's name on it. "This'll cover you just in case, but I need it back after."

"Oh right," Paul says, "I'm twenty-one."

"This ain't New York, baby. You got to be at least that old."

"You never said."

"Never thought you didn't know."

"What about that busboy?"

"Like I said, it ain't his lookout to check IDs."

"How'd you get it?"

"Ask me no questions . . ."

"What about you?"

"I got the original."

"A duplicate might not be good enough if I do get carded."

"The worse can happen is they kick you out. If they do I'll drive you home."

"I'm thirsty from waiting for you to show."

"Here, take mine." Hal maneuvers him into the tiled stairwell close to the entry.

"This juice's loaded with booze."

"You're shitting me."

"I want a cola," Paul says. "And don't slip any rotgut in it."

"You're the only kid I know who'd turn down a real drink."

"That's probably why you called me."

"I'm all ears."

"For insurance. So I can drag your ass home—wherever that is—if you get falling down drunk."

"Plenty guys here'd do that for me. Girls too. Be a line out the door and around the block."

"What else'd they do?"

"That's a long list."

Paul turns to leave.

His sometime buddy nabs him in a loose chokehold. "Second floor before I belt you. There's people to meet."

"Hope none of them's like you."

Hal laughs and heads back out the stairwell.

"Where you going?" Paul says.

"The bar. Some whiny kid bitched he was thirsty."

"Better not forget where I am."

"Don't worry, you won't be alone for long."

Hal's right. But not how Paul thinks.

Two middle-aged guys in shabby clothes and three-day beards are on him soon as he reaches the top stairwell. Unlike the joking Samurai and the nurse, they have serious, feral desire in their eyes. He resents it. The sense he's easy pickings. He's in no mood for the games of such older men. Not men like this.

"I'll bet it's your first time here," the Chris guy tells him.

"Yeah," Walt says. "We'd've noticed."

"I don't go to bars."

"Don't go or couldn't sneak in before?"

Their leering smiles make him want to slam their heads together.

"So how young are you?" Walt says.

"How old are you?"

The man's face darkens. "That's not something you ask adults."

"You're out late," Chris says.

"Friend asked me to come. Said it'd be like going to a carnival or the zoo."

"Which is it?"

"A little of both."

"It's still late for you to be out," Chris says.

"But not too late to be grilled by strangers."

"Oh, you're a smart kid. Got all the answers."

"Just the ones I know."

"This bar's full of good-looking young guys," Walt says. "Prettier than you and with sweet personalities."

"Don't let me keep you."

Chris laughs but Walt doesn't. He must still be pissed about the age question.

Paul excuses himself and enters the gutted factory space where the magic continues. Loud soul music fills the room. It comes from a juke box lit up like a pinball machine. Tables and chairs from another era hug the walls. Rickety torch lamps fitted with amber bulbs soften the look of grimy brick walls and wooden four-by-fours darkened by decades of sweatshop crud. Brown paint shrouds all the windows. A makeshift dance floor in the center couldn't hold another person. Most dancers are in costume, some not.

"I hear it ain't legal," Hal says from behind, startling him.

"Not two guys anyway." Paul takes his cola and gulps down half of it.

"I mean the upstairs. I hear the city ain't okayed it for dancing or anything else. That's why it's always closed, except for rake-it-in holidays."

Paul becomes aware of the floor, how it gives under collective weight. Old boards creak in time to loud music and pounding feet. "Should I be worried?"

Hal smiles and shrugs.

"If I weren't so tired, I'd take you outside and pulverize you. Just turn you to dust and sweep you into the river. Even the bottom feeders wouldn't want you."

"I'd have to be hogtied first," Hal says. "And you'd miss me too much."

They drift to a corner vacated by dancers. There's a large round table on the other side. Two rings of seats encircle it. Men in expensive suits command the inner ring. Paul remembers seeing a few of them outside. They're busy playing cards. Onlookers in the second ring watch the game intently. Hal names them for Paul. There's Penn Station Judy and Mad Alex and Darryl the Chicken Hawk and Flo the Rip and Jan the Man.

"She's always packing a rolled up sock or a dildo."

"A what?" Paul asks and "Oh," after his buddy explains.

"Got straps to keep it on and everything."

"You saw?"

"Her girlfriend Flo's a whore. Turns tricks on the same bed they sleep in."

"What's Jan think of that?"

"She's her tout. Scouts out the men's clubs to see who wants it."

"You sure know a lot about them."

"I boffed Flo a few times. No charge of course."

"How come?"

"She's a good lay."

"I mean why no charge?"

"I don't have to tell you."

"Boy are you full of yourself tonight."

"And every night."

"This crew like their nicknames?"

"You crazy? You don't use them to their faces, especially

Nick the Shark. He's the bruiser dealing cards. I hear he had a guy offed in Vegas. Some drunken clown embarrassed his wife big time. She used to be a guy herself. Performed in a drag show called *The Jewel Box Review*. It's supposed to be world famous. It played the Luxor Follies down Market Street last year. Anyway, this Vegas loudmouth knew her from before. He spilled her beads real loud—right in the casino. Wait'll you see her. Fuckin' gorgeous. I wouldn't turn down a piece of that tail. Not if I could get away with it. Meanwhile the loudmouth who read her got buried in the desert somewhere. Or so the story goes."

"Why's that woman called Penn Station Judy?" Paul asks.

"She hangs out there. I hear she works the afternoon buses going to the city and back. They're half-empty then. She hooks some horny troll waiting at the stop. When the bus comes they get in back. She gives him a hand-job while he pretends to read the paper. She keeps a copy folded in case."

"In case of what?"

"The guy doesn't have one. Geez you're slow tonight even for you."

Paul stares at the dowdy, middle-aged woman with the pasty face and wonders what he's not seeing. "You hear a lot of things about people."

"I get around."

"Sounds like nothing but gossip. Hard to believe at that."

"You don't have to believe for it to be true."

"She ever get caught?"

Hal shrugs. "I ain't her keeper."

"What about the other gamblers?"

"Don't know them yet. But I'd like to. Nick even more. I might have an in with his wifey. We got to talking downstairs. I did some business for her last summer." Hal mimes popping pills in his mouth.

"Why'd you want to know her husband so bad?"

"To learn from him, like an apprentice. Eventually get to play the circuit with him."

"You mean like a professional?"

"That's the idea."

"What happened to you joining the service after graduation?"

Hal gives him a puzzled look.

"Remember in your car last summer? Did I change your mind?"

"Must've been talking off the top of my head."

"You sounded serious."

"I'm more serious about this."

Paul's heard enough about Nick the Shark and everyone else. He can't help thinking of his father's club. How members there have nasty nicknames too. How they gamble their money away. Sometimes argue about it. The parallel disturbs him, the sense he might be in another place where he doesn't belong. He runs his eyes across the group and pulls a face.

"Got a problem?" Hal says.

"I'll bet anything there's a lot of nice people here to-night. Why not introduce me to them instead, or don't you know any?"

Hal takes a step back and turns on his screw-you look.

"If you don't like who I hang with maybe you should go on your own."

"Maybe I should."

Hal heads for the stairwell and downstairs. Paul doesn't follow after. He takes his hurt pride to the shaky dance floor. A slow ballad hits the juke. The scene gets more un-real. A matador embraces his bull. A massive guy in a tutu grinds against a diminutive satyr. Three five-and-dime ghouls lock arms. The women sway in unison, slurring lyr-ics that assault his ears.

"Let's have a go, you and me."

Someone dressed in tight black jeans and a satiny, form-fitting T-shirt takes his hand.

"It's almost finished," he says. But he's drawn into the pack anyway. His arm curls around a slender waist that leads down to subtle curves. His cheek slides against his partner's smooth, soft-featured face. Their bodies press together lightly.

"I love this song," he's told. "Always makes me think of Paris although I've never been there. All I get are promises."

The voice has a sultry timbre. He likes the clean smell-ing red hair with its puckish cut and schoolboy bangs. He

216

can't think what to say. He's having a hard enough time not stepping on small feet shod in penny loafers.

"What's your name?" he asks after giving his own.

"You seem like a sweet boy," Toni says. "You should join my crowd after this."

A fast song with a hammering beat replaces the ballad. He and Toni head off the dance floor. Others push in to claim their spot. Her sling purse gets tangled on a court jester's flailing arm. Paul tries to undo the narrow leather strap. It's hard work. The tipsy clown won't stop bouncing around and cooperate. Guy thinks he's funny. Paul manages to free the purse. He curls his foot behind the dancer's ankle and watches the slow tumble. Bells on the jester's cap jingle all the way down. Other dancers break his fall.

"I saw that." Toni takes his arm and leads him away.

Paul holds a finger to his lips.

"I thought you were sweet," she says.

"I feel bad already."

And he does. Tripping that joker was dead wrong. Something his occasional buddy would do. He feels worse when he sees where she's taking him. Talk about just deserts. The seeming inevitability spooks him. It's like that karma stuff he's been reading about, per Dr. Fabiani's request.

"Your friend asked me to come upstairs and find you," she says.

"What for?"

"To dance with you."

"So I've been set up," Paul says. "And I thought you were sweet too."

"What could be sweeter than aiding a *rapprochement*?"

"I might tell you if I knew what it meant."

"I think you know already."

One thing Paul does know. Hal's clearly enjoying the little trick. His triumphant smirk grates. So does the big chivalry trip he does on Toni to her obvious delight: Standing like a military cadet as she approaches the crowded table. Offering his own chair behind Nick so she can sit near her hubby. Helping her get settled as if she's in a hoop skirt and not a tomboy outfit that makes her look even more feminine in a place filled with over-the-top drag queens.

"Sit beside me," she says.

Everyone in the outer circle makes room for two more chairs so Paul and Hal can bookend her.

Nick offers his wife a fleeting smile. She reaches up and rubs his brindle crew-cut.

"This is Paul," she tells him, "He's a friend of Hal's, and I think he's sweet."

"That's good."

"We danced together."

Nick gives him a hard look. "You didn't step on her toes, did you? She got very sensitive feet."

"I came close a few times."

"But you didn't land?"

Paul shakes his head.

"Good kid." Nick goes back to his cards.

The other players, engrossed in their own hands, pay no attention. Money lies on the table in a sloppy heap. It's much more than Paul's seen at one time. Abandoned cards frame the bets. He has no idea what they're playing and doesn't care. He scans the other onlookers. Except for Toni, everyone's eyes are fixed on the gamblers and all that green. They seem mesmerized. The short busboy comes over to the table. He collects empty glasses after getting an okay from Nick, who asks if the other players want another seltzer. All but one declines.

"I could do with a Yoo-hoo," the bearded guy says. "You got Yoo-hoos?"

"You what?" the busboy says.

"A kid's chocolate drink. It comes in a soda bottle so you know it's fresh."

"Does this look like a candy store to you?" Nick says.

"It's for my stomach. A little prevention in case there's bad news."

"About what?" Mad Alex leans forward, bug-eyed.

"Was I talking to you?" the guy says without turning around.

Alex springs back in his chair.

"Let's cut this short," Nick says. "You got milk?"

"Big cartons only," the busboy tells him. "For mix-up drinks."

The Yoo-hoo guy pulls a face. "I'll have a glass—long as it ain't dated."

"Dated," the busboy repeats like it's a new word.

"You said there was no wait service upstairs," Paul says.

"This table's an exception." Hal sounds smug, like it makes him special sitting there.

"So what about you?" Paul asks.

"What about me?"

"Can't you order something or aren't you allowed?"

"Still nursing this one."

Paul doesn't buy it for a second. "I'll have a cola," he says and waits to see what happens.

The busboy turns to Nick for approval.

"Make mine a G-and-T," Toni says.

"And what about you, Hal?" Paul asks again.

"Said I didn't want any."

"Guess I'm not the only kid who'd turn down a real drink."

"He'll have another of this," Toni says.

The busboy sniffs at Hal's nearly empty glass.

"Is-a-vodka-orange?" His heavy accent fuses the words together.

"I hope so," Hal says.

Nick cocks his head and the busboy rushes off without asking the other spectators, who don't seem to mind. Paul turns to Jan, seated on his left. Her sharp features make for a striking profile. Her glued-on sideburns have loosened and curled a little on the ends. He wonders if she wears them every day like her other accessory, prominently displayed in worn blue jeans that match her denim jacket. He introduces himself in case she didn't hear.

"But I don't know you," she says in a resonant voice. "I never talk to someone I don't know first."

"Isn't that what an introduction's for?" He'd like to know how she touts her girlfriend if she never talks to strangers.

"Don't mind Jan," Flo tells him, "We're studying." She points a delicate, red-tipped finger at the table.

"We all are," Mad Alex says. "Going to compare notes later." He strokes a large wooden crucifix that dangles from his turkey neck. The cross has a scruffy, unclothed porcelain doll tied to it. Paul has a feeling the crucifix isn't only for Halloween.

"I'll switch seats with you, Jan." This from Darryl the Chicken Hawk, busy giving Paul a wall-eyed leer.

"That would be bad luck," Penn Station Judy tells him.

"For who?" Darryl says.

The question seems to befuddle her.

"It's getting awful chatty behind me," the Yoo-hoo sharp complains and everyone falls silent.

"Let's dance again," Toni says to Paul after a while.

"Wait until this hand's over," Nick tells her. "You're bringing me luck."

His words have an electric effect on the observers. They

lean forward with anticipation. If the other gamblers are worried they don't show it. Hal resembles a cat staring at a bird just out of reach. He probably regrets giving up his seat behind Nick, who plays his cards low to the table.

"Paul wants to dance," Toni says.

"I do?"

"Hal can dance with him."

"I don't dance with guys, Nick."

"As a favor to me. Toni's playing lucky charms over here."

Nick's watery brown eyes, set deep in his thick face, display impatience.

Hal shifts out of his chair. "Come on if you want to so much."

Paul lets him hang a little before following. They stand near the dance floor while another ballad spins. He reaches for the narrow waist.

Hal pulls away. "I'm bigger so I should lead."

"You're broader, I'm taller."

"By a couple inches—if."

"Sounds like you need glasses as well as a pair of lifts."

"It ain't like Nick gives a shit if we dance or not."

"I wouldn't know. I'm not the one sucking up to him."

Hal makes to split but Paul blocks him. "You're not pulling this all night."

"That's for sure."

"I mean walking away. You asked me to come, remember? You called out of the blue and asked. You were glad to see me. We were doing great. Then you started up with that sorry crew at the table. Why not fake you're still glad I'm here? You're good at faking. It won't take long since I have to go soon." His voice reveals more emotion then he means to show. His face as well. Hal opens his arms. Paul enjoys the welcoming gesture—or is it one of resignation?—long as he can before starting.

"Figured you'd go in close," Hal says.

"The music's loud and I want you to hear."

"More bitching?"

"That I missed you even though you're nowhere worth it."

Hal laughs. His body relaxes against the other boy's, and they sway awkwardly in place to the music.

"So how you been?" Paul says. "Still in school I hope."

"Yes, Professor."

"And that group home?"

He feels Hal stiffen.

"I cut a deal. I'm there, but not there. Not most of the time. Just when snitches from the city are nosing around. Otherwise I stay at another place. It's unofficial."

"As in your caseworker doesn't know and wouldn't like it if he did?"

"That about covers it."

"How'd you pull it off?"

"Lucked into some primo dirt on the home's operator.

Told you it pays to run with all kinds of people. Never can tell who knows who. Never know what you can learn. Found out the guy got a past he don't want Child Welfare wise to. I'll skip the details. But I let him know *I* knew soon as I heard. Makes him real agreeable when I want to do stuff, like not show up at the home for days at a time. This other dump I live at. The unofficial one. I got it all to myself tonight, know what I'm saying?"

The same mouth that twisted in disdain over dancing with another boy moves across Paul's ear, works its way down his long neck, leaving a trail of confusion and desire. But not too much confusion.

"Is it far, this place?"

"A few minutes in my car."

"Let's leave now."

"Right after I finish with Nick."

"When'll that be?"

Paul feels the shrug and pulls away.

"I want an invite to the next game," Hal says. "Just to watch. Make myself useful somehow. Don't know where it'll be yet or when. Neither does Toni. Or she won't tell me. I'll try and get him alone when they take a pee break or something. Can't ask in front of the others watching. It'll steam Nick. He don't want those bozos sniffing around him on the circuit. They only stumbled into this set."

"You mean like you did?" Paul says.

"Don't go comparing me to—"

Rows of fluorescent lights flicker on above them, casting the dark space in an ugly, glaring, smoke-filled shade of blue. The wailing falsetto on the juke grinds down to a slow bass and stops. Everyone looks around, disoriented by brilliant light. Many complain loudly.

And everything happens fast.

"Those fuckers blocking the stairs ain't in costumes," Hal says.

The largest, oldest cop in the group has a booming voice. It cuts through all the griping when he announces the raid, tells everyone to form a line and have their IDs ready for inspection downstairs. Two cops stand guard at the stairwell, batons in hand. Two others fan out among the crowd and start herding people into a tight, serpentine queue. They work with little resistance. Guys in drag get rough treatment anyway.

"It's only for Halloween, officer," one of them says and flounces his skirt.

The cop pushes harder and the guy almost topples in his wobbly stilettos.

"We got to put a lot of space between us," Hal says.

"Why?"

"Our ID's. You got the duplicate. Can't have two Jerry Pescatores standing next to each other."

"You sure the dup'll be enough to get me out of here?"

"Sure I'm sure."

"I'm not."

"So what can we do about it?"

"What do you think?"

Hal looks him straight in the eyes.

"You told me the dup's good as the original," Paul says. "Or is that only when it's my ass on the line?"

His question goes unanswered as one of the cops moves closer, too close to switch IDs and risk getting caught. At least according to Hal. Paul watches his buddy skulk behind some guys next to him and work his way to the other end, stopping now and then, using the still unsettled crowd for cover.

Through it all the gambling table remains active and serene, except for the nervous onlookers. A thin, young cop walks over. He starts laying down the law. Nick stands and the two melt into the nearest corner, with Nick making the cop walk backwards. His burly form obscures their transaction. It's like the cop isn't even there. A moment later Nick's in his chair seated next to his wife, who's been spotting the table for him. The same cop shoves Mad Alex to the floor. "Sacrilegious cock sucker." He rips off Alex's crucifix and stomps the porcelain doll tied to it. He orders the remaining spectators to stand up and join the growing line. All except Toni. She daintily sips her G-and-T while the game continues.

Paul isn't the only one who notes the exemption.

"Hey Nick! Toni!" Hal calls from across the room. "Can I come over and sit with you again?" He wears an eager smile. One that turns sheepish after his fourth attempt gets ignored and the nearest man in blue tells him to shut up.

Paul finds himself on the first floor and closer to the exit in less time than he expects, considering the line that worked its way downstairs. He takes it as a hopeful sign. They must be letting people out without much hassle. At least those with proper IDs. Some patrons don't make the cut for reasons he can't figure. They're sent to another line, and another cop, who grills them while writing in a large black ledger. They're mostly older, substantial looking men in posh casual dress. They're detained along with some much younger ones who'd given the raiders harsh lip. He can understand the wise guys getting held. But why lean on the compliant others well above drinking age?

He asks the brooding man standing in front of him, a man who looks much like them.

"Hush money," the guy says. "Or they want to get them in the papers or 86ed from work."

"You mean the *news*papers?"

"Sometimes they list names if there's a story." The man's face is full of worry.

"Underage guys too?"

"How underage?"

"Seventeen, for example."

"For example?"

"For a fact."

The man regards him as if seeing him for the first time. "They don't put the names of juveniles in the papers."

"What else won't they do? Would they give the kid a break and let him go?"

"Wish I could say yes but I really don't know."

"That's okay."

"I hope so." The man's smile is more a grimace. He turns away like he can't talk about someone else's problem any longer, needs to focus on his own.

More than ever Paul wants to walk through that door unscathed. But what if he doesn't? Different scenarios race through his mind should the police detain him and tell his parents. At the very least his old man refuses to fill out loan papers for college. Max's been stalling big time. He'd welcome a solid excuse, other than his hatred of forms and lack of parental confidence. His underage son getting caught in a gay bar. That'd more than nail it.

Then again the upshot could be much worse. His parents might decide to give up on him and kick him out. He's rendered a ward of the state, like Hal. The cops tell his school as well. He's expelled and sent to a reformatory, like Hal was. Maybe even a mental institution. Perhaps the same hellhole where Hal worked.

Hal. Always Hal. Some buddy. Some friend.

For the first time since his trek downstairs Paul regards the other boy standing far down the line. Hal doesn't notice. He's too busy talking with some people next to him.

He seems relaxed, as if he were queuing for a bus. He even laughs occasionally. Laughs! And why not? He's got nothing to worry about. With that build and that face he's a shoo-in.

Paul digs into his shirt pocket. He studies the license again, hoping the word "duplicate"—stamped in bold caps—might appear less troublesome than he fears and the birthdate more credible. He examines himself in the wall-length mirror. He looks even younger when scared, finds it impossible to buy the arithmetic. So why'd a cop? Especially that tight-ass handling the review. He sits bolt upright at a table near the bar's well-guarded door, left open to the street. His darkly handsome face remains a sullen mask. He speaks little, and in a hushed tone, with those who come before him awaiting judgment.

The man ahead of Paul gazes longingly at the exit before he's allowed to leave. And then it's Paul's turn. The cop studies the license as if it were a wordy, inscrutable document. He examines the boy's face and form with care, offering no clue to his thoughts. Not that they can be good. Why else'd he take so long? Or is it only anxiety that makes a moment seem endless and the outcome bleak? Paul's muscles ache with tension. He takes a deep breath, lets out a sigh that seems to echo around the room.

The cop looks surprised. Did his face crack a smile before turning smooth as stone again?

"Slipped out," Paul says. "Sorry."

"You should be."

"It was for Halloween."

"What was?"

"Being here. Just came to look at the costumes."

"What'd ya drink?"

"A couple sodas only. I swear."

The cop holds out the license between two fingers like a gambler about to deal a card.

"You want me to take it?" Paul says.

"That depends."

"On what?"

"Whether it's yours or not."

Paul hesitates. He knows it's a test but can't decide how to play it. There was that smile, or something like one. And there it is again! But does it mean clemency, its possibility, or is it a cruel trap to put him off guard and land him with the sequestered group? He can't afford to hold back his answer any longer. More delay could hurt the outcome, if that hasn't been decided already.

He thinks what Hal'd do, what Hal'd want him to do. And then he does the opposite.

CHAPTER 15

PAUL RECHECKS ALL the cabinets in his grandmother's apartment. From her kitchen window he can see Fritz lying on his side in the backyard. The old German shepherd remains shaken. Deep folds crease his black and tan brow. His occasional cries sound like worn car breaks. It's a major effort for him to rise. Arthritic hips drag him up the porch steps. Paul tosses out another treat. Fritz lumbers past it without even a sniff. He sticks his head in the low-set window for more petting and consolation.

What a scene Grandma Mary made over her dog the last minute. Max couldn't bear to draw her away. Lenora refused, complaining of back problems. The delicate task was left to Paul. He knelt beside his grandmother in the yard trying to ease her hold on Fritz. He was shocked by the strength a small, elderly woman could draw on when agitated in the extreme by an extreme event. His reassurances had no effect. For a moment he thought she'd bite his arm. She seemed poised to. He couldn't pull away for fear of tugging her onto the cement path.

"They can't take him," she said instead. "I know what'll happen when I'm gone. You think I didn't hear?"

"But Grandma, you're hurting him."

She stared down at the dog that squirmed in her generous lap. And then it was over. Paul got her upright without much cooperation. Fritz coughed as he dragged himself away. Max retreated to the nearly empty flat. In his absence Mary polished off a can of beer he left on the garden fencepost. Lenora gave it to her, along with a pill she got from her mother-in-law's medicine bag.

"Alcohol?" Paul asked.

"She needs to show up in control," Lenora said.

"But you're not supposed to."

"All the glasses are packed and it's only a few sips. You want her to drink from the garden hose?"

"You're weaving again," his mother says.

"No I'm not, Leo."

"Tell your father he's weaving."

"Dad, you're weaving again."

"What're you weaving?" Mary says.

"There's my favorite sweetheart." Max looks at her through his rearview mirror. Paul can see his father's eyes are bloodshot and wet, and his nose could use a wipe.

Lenora reaches for the wheel. "Stay in the lane or let me drive."

"Her son has to take her."

"Then her son shouldn't've drunk a six-pack."

"It was hard work."

"For the movers maybe. They did everything."

"I don't mean that way."

Lenora relents. She rubs his shoulder and rests her hand there. A little empathy does the trick. Max steers the car in line. He responds better to changing traffic lights and to other drivers tooling along Broadway. "What an avenue this used to be."

"It's a nice street," Mary says. "I learned to drive on it, I think."

"When's my son going to learn?" he says.

"When I can find a patient driver to teach me."

"What are you talking? I was patient with you."

"Then why'd I quit?"

"Because you're a quitter."

"When it makes sense."

"I'm patient, Paulie. I can teach you."

He takes his grandma's hand. Her gray eyes are glassy like her son's, but for a much different reason. Her pink, checkered dress has a small stain from when she knelt distraught in the backyard, clinging to poor Fritz. Her easy demeanor has returned. She seems radiant in comparison.

"You'll be too busy to teach me," he tells her. "What with all the activities they've got up there—remember?"

"Remember." Max sighs. The car swerves a little.

"Of course I remember. Did you pack my swimsuit, Leo?"

"They don't have a pool; that was the first place we looked. And you haven't swum in years."

"But did you pack it?"

"I packed everything."

"Well good then. My boys down in Florida, they have a pool. Bunny has one too. I saw it when I stayed there. It's a new one with a turkey bottom."

"Turquoise," Paul says.

"I can swim at Bunny's when I visit him all summer."

"Bunny has a lot of things other people don't."

"Not today," Max tells his wife. "Don't start on Bunny today."

Lenora's hand drops from his shoulder. She leans against the passenger door as if she might open it. Max veers his way onto the 280 access ramp. He hugs the guard-rail too closely as he ascends the long, steep curve of the single-lane ramp that separates downtown from the more residential wards. The car behind him slows to a wary crawl. Paul holds his breath. Mary smiles at the shrinking street scene below. "It's like that ride we all went on. Remember the world's fair, Max?"

Lenora stares at her husband coolly. She lights a cigarette, blows a lung-full into the car, where it swirls in a gray cloud towards the backseat.

The four-story retirement home could be any large, modern structure built of brick and glass and steel. It sits like a giant series of roseate boxes within a tidy, verdant landscape. Tall oaks and sycamores and evergreens line the property border. A rocket-shaped canopy shelters the path leading from the main street to the entry.

Meanwhile the reception room creates a different impression. One of old-fashioned elegance. Crystal chandeliers sparkle in the sunlight. Landscape paintings in ornate frames hang from copper wires. Flowered chintz and crushed velvet adorn Italian and French provincial furniture. Dense carpeting and dark walnut paneling complete the sense of stepping into another, more refined era. Paul's never seen such a fancy layout before, except in films and illustrated books. He can't believe his grandma will live here. Not when he considers the shotgun flat where she spent all her adult life.

Max walks his mother past the V-shaped reception desk and into the admissions room for some final paperwork. Then it's on to the nurse's station to drop off her unused medications and most recent doctor's report. His son and wife stay behind. They're absorbed by the lobby's grand design.

Paul agrees with his mother. If he had a choice, he'd much prefer to live in a leafy old suburb with all the amenities close by, instead of on a decaying city street. So what if he's surrounded by old people? He likes them well enough. And he'll miss seeing his grandma every day. Their walks with Fritz when the weather permitted. Her behavior towards him devoid of censure, unlike his parents'.

"We should move in too," he jokes.

"Don't think I haven't thought about it," Lenora says. "It's probably the only way I'll get out of Newark now."

"I can't see why Grandma wanted to wait so long. Or how she can afford it."

"Ask your Uncle Bunny over dinner. He's got the power-of-attorney. And while you're at it, ask him how he got that as well."

Mary's one-bedroom "suite" is at ground level. It's in a section designed for residents who can pay the high monthly fee for the illusion of independence. Unlike the ritzy public spaces, the flat resembles a typical garden apartment in its bare-walled simplicity. Three sweaty movers linger at the entrance. They talk with Paul's Uncle Bunny while he tips them based on individual performance. The amounts must vary a lot. One of the men—the older, heavy one—scowls at towering, barrel-chested Bunny, who seems pleased by the response. An antsy staff member hovers nearby. She escorts the movers down the hallway to ensure they leave the building.

"I should've tipped," Max tells his eldest brother.

"Why?"

"You paid for the move."

"No I didn't, Mom paid."

"I did?" She stares at the leather purse dangling from her arm.

"It's all factored in, Ma."

236

"What factory is that?"

Bunny stoops to give her a hug. "Pop's old sweatshop. A little of his pension money."

"So why'd the rest go back in your uncle's wallet?" Lenora whispers to her son as they give the living room a once-over.

"What's that?" Bunny asks her.

"I said you haven't unpacked a single box yet. You and Adelle having a sluggish day?"

Her leather heels muffled by thick cork flooring, Bunny's wife strolls out the bathroom like she's making a grand entrance. She sports a new hair color. It's brown, to match her husband's toupee, maybe? Long bangs and side curls cover most of her small face, recently tightened. She seems more voluptuous than Paul remembers. And nearly full of herself as her husband.

"Does everyone like where I had them place the furniture?" she asks.

"I'm glad you followed my advice," Lenora says.

"Your advice?"

"It'll be just like home," Max says, "after we hang the pictures. What do you think, Ma?"

"I'm not sure about any of that now am I?"

Her family follows Mary around while she goes from room to room, her expression grim as a detective hunting for the smallest clue to an awful crime. Bunny talks up the place as if she's seeing it for the first time and not the third.

She zeroes in hard on the immaculate kitchen, done in amber and avocado. "I can't find one anywhere."

"One what?"

"A mop or broom. Leo didn't pack mine."

"The things she remembers," Lenora says and shakes her head.

"They bring their own cleaning stuff, Ma." Bunny tells her.

"Who does?"

"The housekeepers. They'll keep the place immaculate for you. Do your laundry too."

"But what about that one over there?"

"I'm retiring," Lenora says, "like you. Isn't that a coincidence?"

"Good for you!" Mary tells her and moves on to the stove, where she tries every knob several times. "These fiery things don't work."

"They're not connected," Bunny says.

"And why not?"

"To keep you safe. We don't want you to hurt yourself by accident."

"How am I supposed to cook then?"

"You haven't cooked in two years," Lenora says.

"And you won't have to here," Max adds. "That's what the dining rooms are for. And when you need it, there's room service. They'll bring your meal in on a tray like in a hotel. Like at the world's fair."

"The what?"

Max gets teary-eyed again and rubs his beer belly. His mother opens an avocado-colored door and sticks her head inside. "At least the frigerator works."

"It's for keeping your snacks, the cabinets too. We packed all your favorites."

"What about ice cream?"

"We can get a pint at the café. Or there's a supermarket right down the block."

"I need to have some Dutch chocolate handy."

"Any kind you want, Ma. You're a princess now."

"It's not for me, it's for Paulie."

"Thanks Grandma," he says although he prefers strawberry.

"So where are your kids?" Lenora asks.

"They couldn't make it the last minute," Adelle says. "Too busy cramming for finals. They're both A students you know."

"How could we forget?"

"Dennis has his scholarship to keep up too. But they can't wait to see their grandma first thing summer vacation."

"And to think," Lenora says, "all she had to do was move in here to rate a visit."

Before Adelle can counter, Miss Morgana, the home director, knocks on the open door. She makes a beeline for her new resident. "How are we settling in Mary? Is everything hunky-dory?" She has the tone of a kindergarten teacher the first day of school.

Mary gives the tall, well-dressed woman a once-over. "Aren't you the gal who showed me around here before?"

"That's right, dear. I gave you the royal treatment."

"You remember!" Max says. "She remembers," he tells the others as if they were out of earshot.

"Well then, I need to see everything again before I decide to stay."

Mary and her family eventually get shown around the common areas. Not by Miss Morgana, who only gives a grand tour when there's a sale to be made, but by a lowly aide dressed in a light-blue uniform that makes a rustling sound at her slightest movement. At first the young woman seems glad to be drafted. Mary squints at her ID tag. "I grew up with a gal named Sandy, you know."

"It's Sammie," the aide says.

"No, I'm sure we called her Sandy. Isn't Sammie a boy's name?"

"Not always."

Mary pats her on the arm. "Then you shouldn't worry about it."

Her gregarious mood blossoms in the presence of more strangers. At the small pharmacy she grills a busy druggist about the bottles and medical gadgets that sit behind him on orderly shelves. In the physical therapy room she waylays everyone she sees. "I'm the new one!" she tells a hunched man walking cautiously between low-hung parallel bars.

She follows him back and forth while they talk. Her hand taps nervously on one of the bars. If he feels trapped, the man doesn't show it.

Sammie is a different matter. She starts looking at her watch every few minutes and then at Max or Bunny, then Adelle and, finally, Lenora, who tells her, "She does this sometimes with people in our neighborhood. It could go on for *hours*."

Sammie's eyes grow wide. "But I have to—"

"Go ahead and scoot," Bunny says. "I got the layout down from before."

"Don't show her everything," Lenora tells him. "We need to start unpacking—and it's not like she'll know."

The simple chapel room, with its recessed lighting and red-velvet chairs, is empty. A small podium stands close to the far wall. Glazed pots filled with floral arrangements decorate each corner. Mary shakes her head at the modest space that's absent of any religious meaning. "There should be colored windows with people and animals in them. And where are the statues? I always liked praying to them. Especially Virginia. She was so pretty—except when they wrapped her in purple like a dummy."

"A mummy," Paul says. "That was for Lent."

"For what?"

"The 40 days before Easter."

"But why'd they have to cover her?"

"To keep her from getting dripped on when they repainted the ceiling," he says to avoid the gloomy concept of penance.

She gives the chapel ceiling a review, then stares at the textured beige wall behind the podium. It's bare except for a gauzy spotlight meant to suggest spiritual light. "Shouldn't that other one be hanging up there?"

"The chapel isn't only for Catholics," Bunny says. "It's more like anything goes."

"Oh, I know that one."

"Which one?"

"The song!" She sings the old Cole Porter tune softly, humming in between the many fragmented lyrics, half of which are improvised.

Paul joins in to fill the gaps as he gently walks her out.

She makes quick work of the meeting room, apparently unimpressed by the large oil portraits of board members gazing benignly at a long and deserted mahogany table. Bunny manages to keep her away from the popular music and entertainment rooms. They're well off the main path. But he can't keep her from lingering at the gift store and the beauty shop. Both places are where a lot of the action is on a Saturday afternoon busy with residents getting their hair groomed, and visitors buying overpriced gifts made in the activities area. From there Mary checks out a boisterous group forming in the lobby. They're waiting to take a shopping trip by bus. One Mary wants to go on as well, until Paul reminds her about the unpacking. How she said she wanted everything just so.

"We'll need you there to boss us around," he says to her great delight.

Later in the day they enter the large main dining room. It's designed to resemble an outsized English tea house. The hostess shows them to a table near the courtyard. French doors are open to warm April air that smells of viburnum. Paul recalls the scent from years ago, from his park interludes with Hal, whom he's not seen since last Halloween and doesn't want to think about now.

"So where's the little girl's room?" Mary asks in a booming voice.

"We passed it when we came in," Adelle says. "Let's visit together."

"Oh no we won't. I want to be by myself."

Adelle backs away, her newly smoothed face all flushed.

"I can show you if you want," the hostess says.

"Would you, dear?" Mary and the young woman head for an alcove near the entrance.

"Keep a look out for her, Paulie," his father says.

They've arrived just in time for the weekend "Friendship and Family Hour." One that features a complimentary meal for visitors. A meal prepared, according to the menu, under the watchful eye of Chef Michael himself.

Everyone takes their time looking over the menu, making small talk about the offerings while they wait for Mary.

"It's been forever since I've eaten out," Lenora says.

"They better give us more than an hour. I need a long break from the unpacking."

"It's only a saying," Max tells her.

"No it's not. It's a nice way of telling you to eat fast and leave so they can clean up. You'd think they'd have more staff with what they charge. Look at them. They're all racing around. I bet they double as aides at night. And who eats dinner so early anyway?"

"Old people," Max says. "And the meal's free."

"I'm talking about the big picture, not the meal. And is it really free? What about you Bunny? Do you think anything here's free, or is it all 'factored in' like the moving money?"

"I got to agree with you on this one, Leo. You should've been at the contract negotiations."

"Yeah, I should have. But I didn't know about them until they were over."

"Talk about your piranhas," Bunny says. "I'm glad I packed my lawyer with me. They weren't expecting that bulldog, and having to change some paperwork on the spot. You should've seen the looks on their faces. It was shock city."

"You're always full of surprises, Bunny"

"Here she comes," Paul says.

Mary holds a steady course back to her family but then starts to veer.

"Where you going, Grandma?"

"Next door, over there." She gestures at a nearby table. "I made friends with them back at that other place. The one with all the things in it."

"Which place?"

She performs a jerky motion that vaguely resembles rowing.

"The physical therapy room?"

"It doesn't matter which one," Lenora says. "Let her go if she wants. And if they'll have her. She'll be spending a lot more time with them from now on."

"This is her first meal here," Max says. "It's important to have it with family."

"If it's so important where are her other sons? Oh, that's right. They're both at home in Florida, lounging around their pools."

"Don't start on Vince and Eddie again. You know why they can't come until summer."

"I'm only telling you to get some perspective for a change."

"So anyway," Mary says, "I'm heading off now."

"Of course you are, doll," Bunny tells her.

Max defers to his older brother, though he's clearly unhappy. Paul feels the same way, but for a different reason. He's concerned about how the family, and Lenora in particular, will behave without his grandma around as a buffer, a role Mary unknowingly played during the unpacking, where she darted from room to room perfectly lucid—and very

245

demanding—when it came to her possessions and their placement. He watches her take a seat at the other table as if she were the highly anticipated, but tardy, guest of honor.

"I'm here!" she says. "I'm the new one, remember?"

Startled at first, the three occupants greet her warmly; especially the hunched man who'd strolled between the parallel bars. Mary's new friends must be older than she. Both women have canes hooked to the table. The man keeps a walker close by. They seem enlivened by her company, her loud chatter, interrupted only by the problem of ordering from the menu.

"What's this other one down here?" she asks, tapping her finger on an entrée. And then there's the dessert listing. Its italic print appears to flummox her completely. The man helps with the words she no longer can decipher. After some hedging she makes a decision.

Paul and his family ease their vigilance and order for themselves.

Their food arrives fast on a large, wheeled tray. Two waitresses dole out the dishes as if in competition. Some plates need reshuffling to get them right. The drinks too. Paul wishes the adults hadn't ordered alcoholic ones. Even Lenora has a tall, blazing green daiquiri. "I haven't had one of these since the bowling league dinner last year. My big night out."

Paul remembers the beer she gave Grandma Mary to get that pill down. "Can residents drink too?"

"Only with their doctor's okay," Adelle says. "It's good for morale if they were used to having a drink on the outside. I mean in their homes. Helps them feel independent. That's what the dietitian said."

"How do the waitresses know which ones can drink?"

Adelle looks at her husband.

"They always ask for names," he says. "Like checking someone's ID at a saloon. They keep a list at the bar. No name, no booze."

"But the waitress didn't ask for any of yours," Paul says.

"Whoa, kid! How old do you think we look?"

Everyone laughs at Bunny's joke. The tension Paul felt all afternoon breaks up. At least for a brief while. Until the ID business gets him thinking of Hal again.

"They remind me of *Beat the Clock*," Lenora says about the waitresses serving another table. "You remember that old game show on TV, Paulie."

"Kind of. Don't think I liked it much."

"Me neither. All those contests were rigged, you know. Rigged to make people look dumb. Make them lose against that giant clock ticking in the background. Tick, tock. Tick, tock. No matter how fast they moved, how hard they worked, how much they deserved to win—they'd always lose. What about you, Bunny?"

"Never watched it," he says between small bites of food chewed with care.

"Not even once? It was very popular."

"He was too busy for TV back then," Adelle says. "Too busy building up the business."

"That's because your husband's the wheeler-dealer in the family. The real go-getter."

Adelle beams at the unexpected compliment. Max does the opposite. Bunny stops cutting his steak. "What's your point, Leo?"

"My point?"

"I feel like I'm listening to Ma over here instead of you."

"No wonder. With all the time we spent together, it's almost like I was married to her."

"I know it got a little rough for you the last year," Adelle says.

"A little rough? And you were such a help. I really appreciated the weekly phone calls from you and Bunny. The short weekend visits. Mary loved your vacation postcards from—where was it the last time? The Bahamas? Those cards were so colorful. It was almost like we were there. But I don't get why you always go someplace that has nothing but water and sand. You live on a frigging island. And you got a big pool in your backyard."

"So where'd you go instead?" Bunny asks.

"If I had your money I'd go to Europe. I'd hop a plane to France."

"The bathrooms are filthy over there—when you can find one."

"How'd you know?"

"I was there during the war."

"That was so different," Paul says, "and a real long time ago."

"Not long enough for me. I had the squirts half the time."

"Bunny, stop!" his wife complains.

"It could've been the Army chow," Max says. "I caught KP duty for a while when I was stationed in Texas. You wouldn't believe how some of those guys worked."

"It's always a gamble when you eat out anywhere," Lenora tells him.

"Why'd you have to say that? I better go check on Ma."

"Leave her alone," Bunny says, "she's doing fine."

They all turn her way and watch. Everyone but Max seems reassured by her hearty appetite, her happy expression as she listens to one of the women talk about something that requires a lot of dramatic gesture.

"The kitchen here was spotless when I did my runthrough," Bunny tells him. "All the workers wore bleachedwhite uniforms. And those hairnets and plastic gloves. You wouldn't believe the steam coming from the dishwashers. Nothing could survive that heat." He holds up an unused spoon. It catches bright sunlight coming from the fragrant courtyard. "Look how clean the silverware is. How perfect our meals are. They got special rules cooking for old people. A big list of regulations the size of a billboard. Saw it hanging on a wall. So maybe that's enough about iffy food already. It'll ruin my appetite."

"You're the one who brought up the squirts," Lenora says.

"Can we please change the subject?" Adelle asks.

Lenora shrugs and takes a long swig of her daiquiri. She stops halfway from placing it on the table. "My drink catches light too. And it's so green. It reminds me of ocean water. It reminds me of your new pool."

"What's with you and pools today?" Bunny says. "You got water on the brain?"

"Blame your mother."

"You can't blame Ma for anything," Max tells her. "She's perfect, even now."

"Of course she is. But you heard her in the car on the way over here. She really wants to swim in Bunny's pool. And she expects to come and stay for a long visit. I mean the whole summer. She has her heart set on it, though she might not tell you."

"She said the whole summer?" Adelle asks.

"Like when you finally cut me a break and took her."

"But that was for a couple of weeks."

"Was it? Seemed more like a couple days to me. And I bet the time flew by for you too, didn't it, Bunny? You being her favorite and all."

"That's crazy talk," Max says. "Ma never played favorites with us boys, did she, Bunny?"

"Of course not. She treated us equal."

"Then how'd you get the power-of-attorney all to your-self?" Lenora asks.

"Because her other sons didn't want the responsibility. That includes your husband over here."

"No it doesn't. Straighten him out, Max."

In the chilly silence everyone turns his way, waiting to hear an alternate version. Max looks off to the side instead.

"What did you tell your wife?" Bunny says. "You tell her this whole thing was my idea?"

"I better go and check on Ma, see how she's doing."

Paul watches his father, beer in hand, slouch over to the other table and introduce himself to Mary's new friends. Meanwhile Lenora's turning redder than her son's ever seen before. Her body vibrates like someone about to have a seizure. She grabs hold of the table. For a moment he worries she might upend it like his father does sometimes when they argue. Then she stops trembling. Her face drains of color.

"You could've had money for a real college," she says. "Instead of that half-ass art school you'll be stuck with."

"What money?"

"We could've moved out of Newark on our share."

"Our share of what? Nobody ever tells me anything."

"She's talking about your Grandma's apartment build-ing," Bunny says. "Her and Pop owned it outright a long time. Kept it in great shape. We could make some good bucks if we sold it and divvied up. Some real good bucks. But it looks like we'll have to sign the place over eventually. After Ma's savings and Pop's pension are gone. Once the rents we collect don't meet her expenses no more. When she gets a lot worse. Needs special care. Your grandma's got a strong ticker. The doc says so. He expects she could hang on a while once she's forgotten you and me. Everything. We don't want her to end up in the back building. It's a big Medicare-Medicaid setup. You haven't seen that layout. It's not good enough for our Ma."

"It's good enough for most people," Lenora says. "More than good enough."

"But not for Ma. We want her to check out like a princess, even if she's so far gone she don't know it. All us boys agreed."

"I didn't agree, and I'm the one who took care of her. Not you or Adelle. And certainly not Max. He only cried in his beer."

"But you're not her daughter, Leo. You're her daughter-in-law."

"I'm still owed, especially since I never really liked her."

"Is there anyone you do like?"

After a while Paul tunes out the sniping that becomes a standard rehash of family squabbles large and small. He watches his father at the other table where civility reigns. Max seems to be enjoying himself kneeling in between his mother and the kindly man. He gazes up at them like a round-eyed child being told a story. His chin barely reaches the tabletop.

Chapter 16

PAUL WALKS FROM school to his preferred bus stop. He could wait for a bus much closer to his school, but he likes to walk the streets while they still bustle with commuters who once lived in the city and kept it vibrant into the night. He hates what happens after sundown. The streets grow nearly empty. It makes him feel abandoned as well, bereft of community, the potential for connection. And there's a tense atmosphere this spring. He can't define it. Like something's going to snap. Probably it's only the warm, humid air. It carries a clammy smell from the Passaic River. A smell that always provokes a sense of foreboding, makes him miss the crisp winter air, no matter how cold.

He also uses his favorite bus stop after an evening's visit to the public library. He could wait at a stop much nearer to that white, palazzo-inspired building. But he's often the only person there. He's avoided the corner ever since last summer, after some drunk pulled up in a rusty Chevy, scrambled out, and tried to drag him onto the passenger seat. The man only stopped after a lucky punch landed him on the sidewalk.

So on this gray Friday afternoon, Paul waits with many others on Broad Street. Behind him crowded benches line narrow Military Park. Tall oaks fill the triangle-shaped common with generous shade. They provide the green setting for a massive bronze statue crowded with figures, a statue that pays homage to Newark's war heroes. Across the wide commercial street three of the city's major department stores bustle with shoppers. The middle store, Klein's, he never visits. It's where he and Hal got in big trouble several years ago. And all because of the jacket Hal coveted. Sometimes while waiting for his bus Paul thinks about the incident. Sometimes he freaks when he sees a man similar to one of the security guards who nabbed them. Especially the creep who assaulted Hal and got away with it.

Other times, like almost every night, and despite his best intentions to forget, he thinks about his estranged and problematic buddy. How he'd like to share his grandma's spare bedroom suite with Hal. The suite left behind for Goodwill to collect until Leonora claimed it—along with the otherwise empty apartment—insisting she needed the place to herself a while before Bunny could rent it. Her squatter's maneuver has won old Fritz a reprieve from the big sleep. But it's made family relations worse than ever. And another reason Paul takes his time getting home.

His own problems he brushes aside when he sees the familiar gait of someone with far more worries than he. The Pencil Lady makes her slow way to his end of the long bus stop. Her knees point inward at sharp angles as she walks. They cause her diminutive body to move sideways like a metronome in slow, full swing. Her delicate mouth forms the same smile he always sees on her small-featured face. It's a smile like those in pictures of aged saints celebrated for their kindness; a smile that, in her case, denotes yet another tragic disability.

Some pencils remain in the leatherette cup she carries. She sells them to people who work in the brick-and-sandstone skyscrapers that ring Military Park. He buys a few for a generous sum whenever he sees her. That includes on the bus he takes to school, if she happens to board at her usual stop. He's about to walk over and make another purchase, but stops when he notices someone who seems to be watching her from behind, though it's hard to tell. The scowling, dark-haired man has a dented, lopsided face and bulbous nose. His eyes are sunken. One's a little higher than the other, making it unclear what or whom he's observing. He holds a shiny aluminum lunchbox by its handle, raps it lightly against his leg. He appears tense, angry. Or is it merely the set of his features that leaves this impression on a wary boy whose bus has arrived?

A rambling line swarms in front of the number 18. The Pencil Lady gets swept up somewhere in the middle, a few boarders ahead of the scowling man. Paul finds himself near the line's end that continues to grow with latecomers. The warm bus fills up fast. He stands in the crowded aisle near the uniformed driver and far from the Pencil Lady. She's seated in the back across from the scowling man, who seems to divide his attention between her and his tabloid. He rocks in his chair as if about to spring from it.

Seven stops later the bus idles beneath the gloomy Lackawanna railway bridge built of brownstone. It's no longer a busy stop. Only a middle-aged black woman stands in a corner, smoking a cigarette down to the nub, on the lookout for something other than transport.

The Pencil Lady takes the rear exit out, sidling her way to the curb. She's followed by the scowling man, who may be walking slowly on purpose, keeping a steady distance of several yards. Then again his slowness could be unrelated. He might be tired despite all the nervous energy displayed on the bus. Paul considers the odds of that. He doesn't like them. Before the light changes he makes the grumbling driver open the front door again to let him out. He trails the dubious man, who hasn't changed his stride. Further ahead the Pencil Lady advances past the railway bridge and the 280 access ramp. Opposite them all the stately Episcopal Church reaches for the sky. Forbidding gargoyles stand sentry atop its white spire.

The Pencil Lady turns right at the first narrow side street, still tailed, perhaps, by the scowling man, who definitely has a tail of his own. Paul's never been on Grant Street before. Only one side has buildings. Three brownstone row houses stand among several tenements. The brownstones once housed prominent businessmen and politicos—even a mayor—a century ago, during the street's brief heyday. Certainly no wealthy people would live here now. Not with the grimy, concrete underside of a highway ramp as their front view. And not with neighbors like the scowling man, who climbs the high staircase of the first brownstone mumbling to himself. Nor the Pencil Lady, who totters her way to the last, formerly grand building on the short block, where she stops to talk with someone lounging on the stoop. Someone obscured by the stone railing.

A few pedestrians approach from the opposite direction, their eyes cast down, their expressions preoccupied. All seems well with the Pencil Lady. No need for Paul to linger. No need to have trailed her in the first place, except to satisfy his growing urban paranoia.

He's ready to hop another bus home. But then the person sitting on the stoop jumps up and everything changes. Hal smiles broadly as he digs into his jeans pocket, hands over some money for the remaining pencils. He must make a joke of sliding them behind each ear. The Pencil Lady hugs her chest in evident delight. She holds her empty cup in the crook of her arm, unlatches the small purse dangling from her wrist and drops in the cash. They talk a while more. She makes her way to a red brick tenement towards the end of the block, where the road curves in submission to the rising access ramp.

Hal walks her there then turns back. His expression seems dreamy and reflective until he spies Paul. Then his face becomes a taut mask. People and cars continue to pass.

Neither boy moves. Paul wants his onetime buddy to be the first, but it's not happening. And it probably won't if the past is an example. He takes a step forward, then another, hoping to see his effort mirrored at least once before the distance between them disappears. He gets close as pride allows and waits. He can't help comparing the willful real boy standing before him with the more pliant, easygoing buddy of his nighttime fantasies. Perhaps he should walk away and settle for the idealized Hal, a distorted memory he can use when lonely and horny, then safely put out of mind until someone better comes along. Someone he can trust.

The real boy could prove a big distraction in the off chance they become close again and want to make up for lost time. Paul certainly would, though he needs to focus more than ever. He has a month of school to finish and exams to pass before graduation. And there's his final art project to complete. It's a fragile construct of colored glass shards and metal scraps he's been attaching—with tedious precision—to a mirrored wooden panel. He works on it in the basement of his grandma's building to avoid Max's ridicule.

Despite his growing concern, he moves a step closer, then another. He feels as though he were walking barefoot on his artwork-in-progress, trying to avoid its many sharp edges. What if he's cruelly shunned or worse? Hal could pick a fight about the bar raid last Halloween, though he'd

259

have no right. He might even get physical. And he's become the much superior fighter since their boyhood scuffle years ago. Then again he was such a good guy with the Pencil Lady. Nothing like the punk who robbed an elderly couple with his brother and claimed to hate anyone old.

Nature seems to force the matter with a sudden light shower. Paul'd like to wait it out. Wait Hal out too, still standing, hands in pockets, as if the sky were dribbling sunbeams instead. Should the sprinkle turn to rain, he won't risk damaging the textbooks and class notes he carries in his backpack. The railroad bridge is only a short jog away. He can stay under it until the wet blows over then catch another bus, obsessing about what could've been but for his pride, and the other boy's obstinacy. At least he knows what street Hal lives on. Or does he? Hal might only be visiting. He might—

"You lost or something?"

The words pierce his concentration. They arrive on a hoarse, splintered voice that sounds nothing like Hal's.

"Over here at the window."

A long, sallow face peers through the dark screen. Rings of flesh hang along the man's neck like melted wax on a dwindling candle.

"I said are you lost?"

Paul shakes his head.

"You just like to stand in the rain and get wet?"

He shakes his head again.

"Could've fooled me." The man tries to raise the dusty screen, but it's stuck so he gives up. "You're welcome to come inside if you like, until you figure what you're doing. Name's Ralph by the way."

"I'm waiting for a friend."

"Another boy?" Ralph says eagerly. "Someone who lives on the block?"

Paul shrugs.

"You can sit in here by the window and wait in comfort. I got beer and soda and snacks. Some girlie magazines to help you pass the time." The man twists his head. "Tell him, Billy. Tell him what all I got."

A much younger face, an elfin boy's face, lights the darkness of a second window.

"Tell him Billy."

"He heard you the first time, man."

"Go on and tell him."

"So there's beer and soda and snacks like he said five seconds ago."

"What else I got?"

"Plenty beaver rags too. And other stuff if you're interested." The boy mimics smoking a joint and taking a long drag.

"That's enough, Billy."

The giggling boy disappears from the window. Ralph seems confident, as if his having a dopey kid shill for him provides a good character reference. He pulls a concerned expression a blind guy wouldn't buy. "If you're in trouble or anything, we can talk about it. I'm a good listener. Known for it in fact. I help out neighborhood kids all the time. I might have some answers for you that you never thought of."

Paul glances in Hal's direction, expecting to see him gone. Instead he seems closer than before by a yard or two. Hard to tell how much. The shower—and the towering gray access ramp in the background—create a flattened perspective like in an Impressionist painting. But at least Hal's moved closer. Could it be the conversation's got him going?

"What're you looking at?" Ralph asks.

"Stuff getting wet."

"Guess it was a dumb question."

"No it wasn't."

"The rain'd look much better from a dry place."

This guy's a broken record. But his sleazy pitch might serve a good purpose. Paul tests his theory by approaching the staircase. He rests a foot on the first step and leaves it there.

"I'll open up for you."

Ralph vanishes from the window. And Hal puts on speed. He arrives as the man appears at the front door.

"He's come to see me," Hal says.

"You know you're always welcome too."

"Some other time."

"While you're here I'm ready when you are."

"Maybe later. I'll call you when."

"When!" Billy says, back at the window, his nose pressed against the dusty screen. "When! When! When!" Ralph leans over the stair case. He taps on the screen and Billy's pug nose. The boy withdraws in another fit of giggles.

So does Hal, minus the laughter but with Paul in tow.

"Guy's a major chicken hawk."

"No kidding."

"Likes 'em young *and* straight."

"How's that work?"

"They got to act it, I mean. He's the one who hid me when I was on the lam."

"After you creamed that store guard?"

"Yeah."

"I remember you saying he's a good guy."

"Far as it goes."

"Far as what goes?"

"He can be useful even when he don't know it."

"That sounds familiar."

"Meanwhile you and me got things to settle," Hal says.

"Yeah I know, and I want to. But talking only. No fighting if one guy doesn't like what he hears. We're not kids anymore. At least I'm not."

"You slamming me ain't a great way to start."

"Only telling is all. Going by experience."

"Experience my ass."

"Got a long list in my head."

"You ain't the only one."

"But there's a lot of good stuff on it too. How about yours?"

Hal doesn't answer unless a grunt counts. He stops at the last brownstone where he sat speaking with the Pencil Lady. "Moved into this rooming house a couple months ago. Got a furnished apartment downstairs."

"You mean all your own?"

Hal beams with obvious pride.

"How'd you swing that?"

"Cut a deal with the landlord."

Paul recalls the deals and schemes his friend's had over the years. The ones he knows about. All rank high on his grievance list. "Having your own place must be great."

"You got no idea."

"I been dreaming of one for myself."

"That's because you're a dreamer, not a doer, like me."

"Cut me a break, I'm still in high school."

"Me too."

"You really are full of surprises."

"And you still got a smart mouth."

"Like you don't?" Paul stands in the drizzle, admiring the slyly grinning boy, who seems even more stunning, more touchable, more real, when wet. He drops some strong hints for an invite when none comes.

"Was waiting for you to ask," Hal says. "Remember you did."

"Why? You got the place booby trapped?"

"Only for boobs and cops."

Hal walks down a few stone steps and unlocks the iron gate and the glass-paneled door. He beckons Paul to follow him into a wide vestibule. One that gives the immediate sensation of being haunted. "This is it." All stucco and dark woodwork, the basement apartment seems less a cohesive unit than a series of deeply set entries, like on a prison cell block. A carpeted staircase to the first floor rises at the left. A long hallway leads to two rooms on the right and one at the end.

"Not much to look at up front," Hal says. "But the kitchen in back got plenty windows, and a small courtyard all to myself."

Paul's led to an open doorway and a yellow-painted room filled with natural light. "Sure is a big kitchen."

"The family that built the place was loaded. Even had their own cook who lived down here. So'd a maid. I'll show you where later."

"How'd you know about them?"

"Landlord told me. The guy's loaded too. Got rentals all over. He's kind of a real-estate historian. Knows everything about the city's housing stock, most of which is crap according to him. That's what he calls buildings. Housing stock. Sounds like soup, don't it? We started talking one day when I was hanging on the block. He took a real liking to me."

"A liking?"

"Yeah, that kind. He comes to visit now and then when he can get away from the wife and kids. Said he'd teach me property management. Give me a job if I want. But I got to graduate first. And with decent enough grades to prove I'm serious about my future."

"Think you will?"

"Been holding my own."

"Me too," Paul says. "I got a grant for the art institute connected with my high school. I'll be starting in September. It's vocational but really good. Like Pratt or Cooper Union. Except it's not accredited like them."

"If you say so," Hal says. "It ain't like I'd know the difference."

Or care much from his bored expression. He pulls a chair out from under a round wooden table, on which lie a small stack of textbooks and an empty red bowl. "Park it here a while and give me a hand."

Paul looks at the top book on the pile. "Got to warn you, I'm only making C's in calculus. And I'm sure my teacher's grading on a curve."

"The math we'll be doing's a lot easier." Hal gets a couple sodas for them to drink. "Stay put," he says like it's a joke to take seriously. He leaves the room and returns with a rectangular-shaped package. It's wrapped tightly in thick brown paper. From a cabinet over the sink he gets two small kitchen scales. He sits them near the bowl and opens the package he placed inside it, exposing a vegetal brick that resembles frozen spinach set out to thaw until brown and dry.

"That what I think it is?" Paul squirms in his seat.

Hal grabs a bunch of small plastic bags from a counter drawer. "And some of these for me and you to fill up for Ralph."

"Me? I don't know about that."

"Don't be so square. I figured you don't smoke. Not yet anyway. But at least you can play stock boy while we chew the fat."

"I mean I don't know how to."

"Nothing to it."

"Then you can play stock boy alone."

"Four hands are better than two, even when two of them's yours. We can catch up while we bag."

"Or we can catch up while I watch."

Hal grabs a couple curved white plates off a wooden dish rack above the table. He slides one in front of Paul and takes a seat next to him. He crumbles some of the fragrant brick with his fingers. His large hand hovers over the loosened grass like an elegant bronze claw. "Take about this amount and spread it on your plate. Clean out most of the seeds and twigs like this. I get bitched at if the bags got too many. Then you put this much weed in the scale bowl.

Keep adding a little at a time. When you got a lid pour it into the bag."

"Where's the lid?" Paul says.

"It's an ounce of grass, altar boy. See where the little arrow points on the scale?"

"Yeah, it says 'one', not lid. And I'm no altar boy."

"If you were you'd already know. Like that kid you saw at Ralph's window."

"Billy?"

"Fifteen and a stoner. Ralph knows plenty altar boys, current and former. All that incense they breathe at church must prime them for weed. Smells heavy like pot but don't get them high. Got to be frustrating. That and having the priests always nosing at their crotches. Billy lives in the group home where I'm supposed to live at. It's right around the corner on Spring. Real convenient for when I got to show myself for state inspections. Plenty convenient for Ralph too."

"You sell to those kids?"

"I sell to Ralph and some others guys like him. They share it with whoever."

"You mean as a come-on."

"What they do with it's their business. My only lookout is building a solid cash cushion."

"You still sell pills too from that hospital you worked in?"

Hal pulls a face. "That gig's long over and we ain't talking about it."

Paul slides away his plate. "When you joked about your apartment being booby trapped, you said for cops."

"And boobs. I said boobs first."

"Aren't you worried you might get caught dealing?"

"I'm no dealer. I'm a retailer."

"What's the difference?"

"I buy from a middle man who's got a steady job and a safe place to score. I never sell to dealers. Especially street dealers. Just the guys I told you about. Street customers'd mean more risk. I like to work careful."

"Would your being careful make any difference to the police?"

"Since I got out of Hollyfield, the only time I had cop trouble was Halloween. You remember Halloween, don't you?"

"I remember almost getting arrested," Paul says, "because of that damn card you gave me. And because I was way underage."

"But you weren't nabbed, were you? And you didn't stick around like a good buddy to see if I was."

Paul waits to hear more, but he's left hanging. "So were you?"

"Came damn close," Hal says. "That closet case running the exit line. He stuck me in the group headed for the paddy wagon. I'd be back in Hollyfield—or someplace worse—if Toni hadn't spotted me on her way out with Nick. She threw me some last-minute pity. Talked her old man into squaring me. I owe her big time. Know how I'd like to pay her back too if I ever see her again."

"That same cop made me sweat," Paul says, "but he let me go."

"Well good for you. But when I showed him the driver's license I was using, he compared it to the card you left with him. The prick sneered at me like I was dirt. Said I was corrupting a minor giving you my duplicate to get into a fag bar."

"But you're underage too."

"I sure don't look it though. And if he took me down the station and found out both cards were pinched—and he would've—I'd be set for a two-way screw."

"You never told me they were stolen."

"You didn't ask hard enough. Just like you always do when you don't want to know."

"He took that card from me. I didn't have a choice."

"You must've had an idea what he'd do with it. And you still didn't hang around to see I got out okay."

"Like you would've."

"Damn right."

"Because it'd be all your fault if I got arrested?"

"No one forced you to come in the first place. No one forced you to do anything we ever did together."

"That's not true."

"I don't see no marks on you."

"You always made like we wouldn't be friends if I didn't go along."

"That ain't force."

"It is when one of us gives a damn."

Hal sits back in his chair, arms crossed, and looks at the other boy with what seems like regret. Whether for inviting him or for getting him in trouble, Paul can't tell. He takes back the plate he slid away.

"So, like this?" He teases a small tuft of grass from the pile. Hal's expression seems to say so much more than yes. But what exactly it's hard to tell.

He walks out of the john to find the main room dark. Slender bands of light from the street frame three opaque window shades, fully drawn. He tries to remember the layout. In his state it's hard to recall. He backtracks and reaches for the bathroom light switch.

"Leave it off," Hal says. "We don't need it."

"We did a few minutes ago."

"Yeah well, that was then."

Paul feels his way around a bureau and some clunky bookcases put together with planks and cinder blocks. The curio cabinet, distinguishable only in outline, he remembers clearly. It's filled with stuffed animals and other junk prizes. Ralph told him they're mementos from his years as a carnie gamer. Most of the man's other furnishings hug the octagonal walls as well, except for a large, iron-framed bed that dominates the space.

"Watch it," Hal says from close by. Paul feels an arm

271

around his waist. He's shifted a few feet to the left. "Stand here. You were heading for Ralph's set."

"Don't remember a TV there."

"It's a projector."

"Don't remember that either."

"He got it out to show a movie."

"He could pull up a shade until he's ready."

"Why don't you boys take your shoes off and lie on the bed?" Ralph says. "Plump up the pillows. Make yourselves comfortable. I want you to have front-row seats."

Hal takes Paul by the arm. It's all the encouragement he needs.

Once they're horizontal Ralph turns on the tiny projector light.

"He could've done that before," Paul whispers. "Why all the mystery?"

"The dark's a part of his thing," Hal says. "He's got to go step-by-step a certain way or it don't work for him."

"What thing?"

"His porno thing."

"Is that what he's showing?"

"Yeah."

"Never seen one before."

"The guy he buys from was out of *Snow White*."

"I feel even dizzier lying down."

"It'll pass. Then you'll feel nothing but stoned."

"How's that supposed to feel again?"

"You'll know when. Then you can tell me about it."

Paul hopes it's a lot better that feeling barely able to move or think. "You said we were only going to drop it off."

"We couldn't turn down smoking my own stuff. It ain't sociable, and it'd look suspicious—wouldn't it Ralph?"

"*Very* suspicious."

"But we've done that. So why can't we go back to your place?"

"You don't want to miss this show," Hal says.

The small projector light allows Paul to see better. Ralph keeps fussing with the film and some knobs. Cartwheels squeak whenever he repositions the portable machine. Clicking sounds from the projection reel echo in the room. A spectral square of light emerges on a bare wall opposite the machine and the bed. It's a gray light with lots of squiggly speckles. The streaks race to the ceiling then vanish.

Blurry figures soon replace them. Two men and a woman. Trashy looking with long, greasy hair. Their conversation seems eager, but there's no sound to know for sure. Mostly the men talk while the blonde woman nods like a kewpie doll with a spring neck and a hollow head. Ralph's hound dog face appears in eerie shadow. "Clipped out the credits," he says. "And I spliced another reel to this one, so you can go long as you want."

"As I want?" Paul says. "When it's over it's over."

"Not at your age."

"I must be stoned now because I don't know what we're

talking about." His confusion sends Hal on a laughing jag. Paul joins in despite not getting the joke. All the laughing makes him boiling hot and he says so.

"You're overdressed is all." Ralph flaps his robe open. It's not a pretty sight. "Hal's overdressed too. Aren't you Hal?"

"Like for a blizzard," Hal says although he's only in street clothes like Paul. He pulls off his shirt and slides off his pants. "Your turn, buddy boy."

"I'm cooling down."

"You'll get cool faster this way."

Hal kneels beside Paul and slowly unbuttons his shirt, undoing his jeans and zipper and lowering his pants to knee level. He splays the shirt open and hikes up the T-shirt beneath. Gently he rubs the naked stomach in a circular fashion. "This is how you put an alligator to sleep. I saw it on TV. You keep rubbing and rubbing until they doze off and get stiff—just like you!"

"Touch it," Paul says, not caring that Ralph's in the room, surprised but not objecting when the man straddles him in a flash, head bent low, offering another kind of touch not asked for.

"Watch the film and enjoy yourself," Ralph says. "That's all I want you to do."

"That's not all you want."

"Let him," Hal says. "I'll take good care of you the whole time."

Ralph gets down before the go-ahead's official.

Paul looks over the man's bobbing head and at the film. On her knees now and naked, the woman's getting nailed doggie style by one of the guys. Meanwhile she's giving head to the other fellow, who reclines like a pie-faced king on a throne of cushions.

"This porno crap's not for me," he says. "You know that."

"Said I'd take care of you, didn't I?" Hal's kisses have their intended effect. They erase Ralph from the scene, help Paul focus instead on what he yearned to have happen in another bed, in another room, and with a different kind of friend.

CHAPTER 17

HE HESITATES ENTERING the building he vowed less than a month ago never to see again. The front door opens before he's about to turn away. His host stays deep in the hallway as if he doesn't want to be seen from the street, not saying a word this time, not trying to persuade. Only watching Paul make his way into the room.

"Take a seat."

"I'd rather take what I came for and get started."

Ralph tosses a set of keys at him.

"Where'd you get them?" Paul says.

"From the guy who runs the group home. The place where Hal's supposed to live. Hal called him and said to give over. The guy was glad to. Said he didn't want to get involved. Good thing Hal cut another set in case."

"In case of what?"

Ralph shrugs. "They didn't come from me if anyone asks. And I don't know nothin' about nothin'—which I don't."

"I'll tell him what a pal you are."

"Listen kid, I got to be extra careful on the outside chance."

"And you think I don't?"

"I'm older than you and I got a past."

"You're a lot older than me, and I'm graduating next week." He glances at the messy bed sheets, the projector only half-hidden in a closet. The thing's probably still warm. And this joker claims he has to be careful. "You sure he didn't say why all the secrecy?"

"I gave you everything he told me right after he called. Want to hear it again?"

What Paul wants is to race out the room with its carnival mementoes, the smell of spent weed and sour bedding. But he needs assurance he has everything right, and from this doubtful, secondhand source. He unfolds the long list he penned while resting the phone against his neck, listening to the uneasy voice on the other end. "By the way, don't call my home again. I don't care what it's about."

"Hal gave me your number. It ain't like I looked it up in the book." Ralph grabs the notebook paper. It's jam-packed on both sides with tiny script. "Did I say all this?"

"I added some questions so I wouldn't forget."

"These ain't some." He hands back the list. "Better you should read it to me. You write like a goddamn doctor."

A car idles near his destination. He's sure it wasn't there before. Two big guys crowd the front seat with their muscular bulk. They meet his gaze then turn away. Was that a reflection on the rear window or a flash of movement in the back seat? Maybe a pale face sinking to the floor?

Paul's imagination veers from undercover cops on a stakeout to dodgy characters lying in wait. He wants that ride gone before he risks going inside. He strolls past it and around the block, kills time at the small grocery store on Spring Street, practicing his Spanish with a friendly young clerk. He buys a large soda, has the clerk bag it for added effect on the street, where he plays the tired local, inching his way home after some late-night shopping. He keeps his head straight while sizing up other pedestrians. They do the same to him, a normal response that ordinarily wouldn't alarm.

But at least it's gone, the car.

He doesn't hesitate, climbs the staircase like he owns it, wishing he had a rearview mirror attached to his head. He squints past the muslin curtain that covers the door window. It's all clear in the hallway. With some jiggling the key turns.

He walks through the long passage to another locked door near the back. One that leads to the basement. He barely has it open when he hears movement overhead. Two people for sure. He closes up behind him and sits on the second step. His heart thumps along with the footfalls until there's silence. He makes his guarded descent. He never got a good look at the flat during his one and only visit. Now he has to search an unfamiliar room in near total darkness, per Hal's instructions. He checks out the windowed front door. Doesn't see anyone lurking in the shadows, watching. He runs his hand along the rough walls until he finds the passage he needs to enter—if he's got the right one. And he has. A tiny red light on the boiler shines a cautionary beacon. The squat machine resembles a big octopus at the bottom of a murky sea. Long pipes rise from its base like giant, searching arms. They invade the room's unfinished ceiling in every direction, sometimes crisscrossing in ways that seem random.

The coded message better be right. It said to look where Hal once laid a girl in Hollyfield. Twice Ralph asked him what Hal meant. Like Paul'd tell if his buddy didn't.

He shoves off his backpack and walks behind the boiler searching for the likely spot. A spot no one but Hal'd think of. He checks the machine for a maintenance hatch. Nothing doing. And much too obvious anyway. He pictures Hal in that school, lying on a discarded blanket with the girl he snuck in, catching a few moments of pleasure. Ceramic tiles compose the fire wall. He taps on the low ones, listening for any variation. It's a tedious process that leaves his knuckles sore before he finds one. Well off to the side. A hollow, muffled noise from behind the corner molding that's shaped like a wide, inverted V. The tile gives under pressure but has a snug fit. He can't dislodge the piece with fingers alone. He works his way out the boiler room through the hallway past the bedroom he's never seen and into the kitchen. In his haste he pulls out a cabinet drawer too hard. Forks, spoons and knives sound like chiming bells when they hit the floor. The drawer slips from his grip. It barely misses his foot. His reflexive yell echoes in the room, rolls in a wave down the hallway and back again.

Every sound in the building seems to stop in response to the clamor. For minutes he makes like a statue. Any hint of trouble and he's ready. Ready to escape through the kitchen door empty-handed and into a tangle of backyards with high fences. He half wishes for a reason to flee. None occurs. So it's off to the boiler and the obstinate tile that reminds him of the boy he's helping. If Paul's guessed right.

His knife of choice has a thick blade. He hopes it won't bend and become useless. He has two others in reserve. The thin crack along the grouting resists his prodding at first. Then he finds the sweet spot. Dead center on top. His improvised tool makes a hissing sound as it slips in. The V-shaped tile flips onto the floor. It stands like a miniature tent before an opening too dark for appraisal. But clearly there. He draws back and waits should any vermin scurry out. He eases his fingers inside. Something falls on his hand and he withdraws fast. He barely can make out a form. One that, to his relief, doesn't appear in nature. He holds his breath and tries again, removes a small, opaque plastic bag. It's sealed with masking tape. Plenty of it too. He slides the bag into his backpack between some clothing.

In his head he's good as gone. But he freezes at hearing a noise quite different from the others he monitored, often to crippling effect, while on the hunt. This sound came at basement level. It's one he's heard before. Must be that large round key. The one Hal used to open the security gate out front. He recalls the unique crunching the tumblers made as they seemed to resist falling in place. The gate hinges complain as well. Now another key. This one unlocks the windowed door that closes with a whoosh and a click.

A ceiling light from the hallway reaches partway into the boiler room, casting the furnace and its tangle of pipes in dramatic shadow. Someone walks past. Someone with a man's tread. His mind races to Ralph first. Maybe that creep was lying all the time. Maybe he was biding his time, waiting for the stash, or only its hiding place, to be discovered so he could—

"What in hell's all this!"

The nasally voice coming from the kitchen nixes his Ralph theory. Hal's name is called repeatedly. Footsteps land in the hallway again. They veer off, probably to the bedroom, then fade back to the kitchen.

He hears what must be the silverware being thrown into the sink one-by-one. They make a clatter against the stainless steel nearly as bad as when they crashed to the floor en masse. There's a sense of familiarity and ownership about the angry, repetitive gesture. Must be the landlord Hal told him about. The rich married guy who shows up when he wants a little action.

Paul decides to use the noise for his escape. He fears the landlord, or whoever it is, may want to inspect the entire basement to see what else might be amiss. He knows he would. But how to flee without detection? He won't risk the long staircase from which he descended. The front door. Surely it's the quickest way. To hell with the strong warning not to use it. To hell with Hal too.

The kitchen racket may end at any second. Time to act.

He rises off the floor backpack in hand. He pokes his head out the boiler room far enough to see with one eye. The wide staircase blocks his view of the kitchen entry behind it. Good thing the obstruction works both ways. He's grateful for the floorboards that don't announce his steps, and curses the ones that might. Their mild squeaks prove no competition for the ritual clanging in the kitchen. The din has an obsessive tempo. He tries to match it with his tread. He does well enough to reach the front door without notice. He opens it with a swift action meant to keep the hinges quiet. Heavy and old and much exposed to the elements, the security gate requires more finesse. The clanging suddenly stops. He grabs the latch. He turns it but doesn't exit. Should he wait for the masking noise to continue, or have the gate announce his departure before he runs into the uncertain night?

Water that flows through old kitchen plumbing settles his quandary. The pipes make a strong whooshing sound. He shuts the door while swinging open the security gate.

He walks up the steps and turns right. Then he stops. Better he should take a circular route and avoid Ralph's building. He pivots left and onto tiny Spring Street. Then it's another left at even smaller Clay. A few minutes later and he's on Broadway. He makes a point of standing in front of a busy Puerto Rican restaurant. Customers spill out the entrance. Some have a drink in their hands. They're in a festive mood. A middle-aged couple dances to the heavy percussion music that pours out the open door.

Finally he's caught a break this evening and doesn't have to wait long. A 27 bus heading north to Mt. Prospect tools his way. He flags it down with both hands and takes a seat across from the driver.

CHAPTER 18

THE LAST STOP leaves him at the Belleville township line.
He crosses the street and enters the narrow strip of park. He
sticks to the well-lighted path that follows the Second River
westward and hugs the right bank. It's a longer, more cir-
cuitous route than he took with Hal years ago. But he's
unsure about the short-cuts he could take. And he doesn't
want to challenge his erratic sense of direction at night,
when even the familiar seems new and threatening.

A small hill offers a good vantage point. He climbs it
and relieves himself beneath a willow oak. The tree con-
ceals him behind cascading branches thick with leaves. Its
trunk is marred by lover's initials. He counts the vows of "4
ev r" when not glancing about like a nervous dog with its
leg raised. He doubts a single pairing lasted more than a
season. If that.

Another quick detour takes him to the Old Quarry. The
baseball diamond there has drinking fountains. He chooses
the one near the outermost bleachers. Some rowdy teenagers loiter at the other end of the expansive field. They're
quenching their thirst as well. But from a few bottles con-
cealed in paper bags they pass around. He can hear their
slurred shouting from the diamond. Some kind of wager

made. All at once the boys climb the towering, chain-link fence behind home plate. They're so plastered they barely seem able to hold on, much less ascend. One falls off laughing a few steps into the contest. The others reach their goal, then immediately start arguing about who came first. They ask the kid lying flat on the ground.

"How the fuck should I know?" he yells back.

Paul takes off at a steady pace before the climbers begin their descent. If they can't resolve the issue they might ask him to judge, insisting he witnessed the result. Which he did. They could harass him, maybe worse, for the fun of it, to help fill their night with fresh excitement. He's almost in the wooded area that hugs the open field. Belated calls reach him. Orders to return. The last few packed with curses. He ignores them all, doesn't put on speed, certain he can outflank this drunken crew with ease, disappear into the verdant night before they make it across the diamond, much less the back field. A brief undercover check reassures. The boys make no effort to follow. Instead they're busy kicking something on the ground. Probably their buddy who fell.

He moves westward along Mill Street, a major through route for cars and pedestrians. It's flanked on the right by a fenced-in golf club. Somewhere close to the south there's a footbridge. That'd get him across the river quicker. But he can't recall its exact location, and he's not keen on backtracking even a little. Meanwhile the wide street offers re-assuring lights and some late-night traffic, including a Belleville police car that slows as it approaches. He gives the officers inside a friendly salute and they ride past. He's never seen cops patrolling the park before. Why'd it have to be tonight?

He puffs his way up the hill to Franklin Avenue. Once again the grand park narrows to a green sliver. It ends at the desolate expansion lot of the Clara Maass Medical Center. He makes a U-turn in the lot and reenters the park. This time he takes the only walkway that follows the river's left bank. He turns off the neglected path where the landscaping between it and the river widens. A dense wall of trees and bushes obscures anything—and anyone—behind it. This must be the place. If not, he can't think where else to go. He heads for the water, his footsteps amplified by new undergrowth and crisp duff. Similar sounds come from his right then stop. He advances a few steps more, hears the same crackle and rustle. Their direction shifts behind him, and closer, as if he were being circled.

He crouches behind a small rock formation crowned with thick bushes.

"Hal? Is that you?" He feigns a deep voice. Perhaps whoever's out there hasn't glimpsed his slender, youthful form.

The words seem to have a magical effect. Hal's face and hands materialize from the darkness. His solid body, dressed in black, gathers definition with each slow step. In scant moonlight he looks frazzled. Years older. His face full of worry—and even more beautiful for it. He moves with a slight limp. "Sure took your time getting here."

He smiles in a way Paul takes as deeply felt thanks. His long embrace ends with a lingering kiss on the neck. "Find the stash okay?"

"You're lucky I remembered where you took that girl."

"Any trouble getting it?"

"None," Paul says not to worry him.

"And you got in and out how I said?"

"Exactly."

"So where is it?"

"The main compartment." Paul slides off his backpack and hands it over. Hal digs into the bag, finds his stash packet between some underwear and socks and a shirt.

"What're these for? You want to come with me?"

"Thought you might need a change of clothes."

"Like I'd fit in yours anymore."

"They're my father's."

"I'd go bare-assed first." Hal drops the backpack and embraces Paul again. "It's a joke, sourpuss. Lighten up. I always keep emergency threads in my trunk. I'm wearing some now."

"You have your car?"

"Behind the hospital at the new construction site. How'd you think I got here?"

"Same as me. Imagined you running away from someone and—Hey!"

Hal ducks behind the rock formation, dragging his
buddy with him. "You think someone followed you?"

"No."

"You sure?"

"Absolutely."

"So what'd you just say?"

"I meant *you*, not me. Thought you had someone hot on
your tail."

"Why'd you think that?"

Paul grabs the folded list from his pocket and hands it
over.

"Who asked me to do all this? Who gave Ralph instructions only I'd understand?"

"Didn't trust that old chicken hawk with my stash is
all."

"I don't deserve a bullshit answer. Not after tonight."

"Only doing you a favor."

"That'd be a first."

"Inside out, that's how I know you. Don't want you to
worry about me."

"I wouldn't've come otherwise."

"When I'm gone for good, I mean. You know I'm no
letter writer."

Paul had this scenario in the back of his mind from the
start, along with far worse ones that drove him to his goal.

He kept them in check until now. Until he saw his buddy again. Heard how things'd be. He thought he'd feel awful when it came down to it. But he doesn't.

"How bad is it?" he says. "And why the limp?"

"It's no big deal."

"Yeah, sure."

"The limp I mean. Sprained my ankle a little when I ran off."

"From what?"

"A fucking gun and the nut-job who held it."

"A gun?"

"You said you wanted to know."

"Show me your ankle first."

"It's nothing."

"Yeah, but I'm not ready to hear about the other thing. A gun!"

"Told you I know you inside out." Hal sits on the ground and leans against the smooth, mossy rocks. He hikes up his left pant leg and rolls down his sock, revealing a compression bandage. "All taken care of."

Paul unlaces the shoe and pulls it off, along with the stretched-out sock.

"What're you doing?"

"You put it on wrong. Didn't you read the damn box?"

"I kind of had other things on my mind."

Paul gently manipulates the ankle. "How's this feel?"

"What do you think?"

"How long's it been sore?"

"Since last night."

Paul makes him bend the good leg so the knee's high. He sets the other calf on it for easy access to the bandage. "Just relax while I fix this."

"Wish I could."

"Count your money. I bet that'd relax you."

"Don't need to."

"Maybe I lightened the stash and replaced it with newspaper."

"No you didn't. That's one thing I'm sure of. It's why you're here. Besides I marked up the tape special. I'd see right off someone opened it."

"Aren't you a clever guy." Paul removes the fanged bandage clip and sticks it in his shirt pocket for safe keeping. He unravels each layer of the ill-fitting compress, lifting the calf up and down like a lever. "You're lucky. It's not swollen or even discolored."

"If I was lucky I wouldn't've hurt it in the first place."

"There's some sandwiches and juice in my pack. Ralph didn't know how long you been hiding out."

"Since last night," Hal says, "though it seems like forever. Caught a few hours' sleep in my car. If you call it sleep. Parked behind the old Tiffany factory after all the shit happened. Come morning I washed up at the visitors' center in the park. Some broom-pusher came in on me while I was half naked. Started bitching in Pidgin English,

'You no allow. You no allow'. I tossed him a couple bucks and he waddled out. Later I drove over the bridge. Had some breakfast at the Lyndhurst Diner. Had my supper there too. A big one. The place is far from where it happened but a quick drive to here. Got a rep for being a cop hang-out."

"And that's a good thing?"

"If you want to dodge people who avoid them."

"Aren't you one of those people now?"

"The cops don't care about me." Hal turns his face away when he says it.

"That guy with the gun. Does he care?"

"Not a bit." Hal goes limp against the smooth rocks and shuts his eyes. His tongue dangles from his mouth.

"That's not funny. And keep your foot up until I'm done."

"You see me laughing?"

"No, but you're shivering." Paul reaches into his backpack and pulls out his father's shirt. He drapes it on his buddy.

"Being cold ain't why." Hal pulls it off. "I get the shakes from nowhere sometime. Or when I think too hard about last night. They been getting better since the first time.

"You should've seen me at the diner the morning after. I was eating breakfast in a corner booth at the quiet end. My mind a bombed-out blank. Suddenly the tabletop started vibrating. I'm thinking it's an earthquake. Then I see nothing else's moving. Only my legs. Couldn't keep them from dancing around. Before I knew it my whole body trembled. My head pounded. My eyes teared up. Thought I was having a fit. Spat out a mouthful so I wouldn't choke.

"The shaking stopped nearly soon as it began. I felt calm again. Even hungry. Ordered up another plate and looked out the parking lot. Instead of cars and blacktop I saw this place. The river. The trees. The same flat rock we left our clothes on the day we washed in the water. That's when I figured what to do. Called up Ralph from the pay phone outside and gave him my game plan. He didn't want to help at first. Said I'd have to drop a dime on him if he didn't. Tell the cops about all the young chicken he's been doing. He came around quick after that."

"All done." Paul shows his handiwork.

"Nice job, doc. Where'd you learn?"

"Had a sore ankle a couple times like most kids."

"Guess I ain't like most kids."

"Lucky for them."

"Fuck you." Hal laughs for the first time. He slides his sock over the bandage and then his shoe. "I'll test it later."

Together they lean against the rocks. Their arms touch. Paul takes his patient's hand. "About last night and that dead guy. I got to ask—did you do it?" The quiet seems endless, interrupted only by rapid breathing that isn't his. "In self-defense, I mean," he adds. But mostly to assure himself.

"I never touched the piece," Hal says. "Didn't know until the creep pulled it on me. Andy saw first. After he gave the special hand signal and we got out his car. I was busy opening the trunk for the delivery."

"Who's Andy?"

"My supplier. He's a middleman for another middleman. A guy who's well-connected but don't like to get his hands dirty. So Andy said. He took me along last night for the first pickup with a new contact. The connected guy made the deal. 100 pounds Colombian gold it was supposed to be. And I'd get five of it just for keeping him company. Andy said I could sell primo weed like that to professional types for big money. Businessmen, lawyers. Said he'd introduce me to some. See how I handled myself around them. Maybe we'd partner up."

"The guy with the gun," Paul says, "what about him?"

"That's the only thing the fucker did bring. There was no weed. It was a setup. A rip-off plain and simple. And there were two scumbags waiting for us at the parking lot. Both of them carrying."

"Carrying what?"

"Man, you're so..." Hal shapes his hand like a pistol and aims at Paul. "One on Andy, the other on me. You can't imagine having a gun in your face and some nut-job hissing, 'turn it over, turn it over'. Guy had crazy eyes like a hophead. Like that loony tune who tried to shaft me back in Hollyfield."

Up close, even in the dark, Paul can make out the knife scar on his friend's neck. He reaches for it with his free hand. Warm blood moves underneath. "Never thought I'd be glad to see this again."

"You almost didn't," Hal says. "That scumbag lost it after his partner counted the cash Andy forked over. Started barking there should be more for 100 pounds Colombian.

"'What're you talking about?' Andy told him. 'It's all I was given'.

"'You're holding out', the nut-job kept shouting.

"'But you didn't bring any,' Andy said, which was the worse way to put it. Only made the wacko think we *were* holding out. He got in front of his partner and shoved the gun at Andy's chest, growling for the rest. Andy freaked and pushed the gun back and up. That's when the thing went off. Blew a big red hole through the guy's jaw. And a bigger one out his head. The blood squirted all over his freaked-out partner, who jumped into his car screaming about payback."

The trembling begins anew. Paul grabs the discarded shirt and covers his buddy again. "Keep it on this time. It'll help."

"Never heard tires screech so much," Hal says after a while and in a small voice. "Guy almost ran over us when he backed up. And he meant to. But we dove behind Andy's ride in time." He pats his ankle. "That's how I got this."

"Did anyone hear?" Paul says. "Or see?"

"Don't think so. Not in that dead factory strip. Andy tore through the potholed lot and pedaled it to McCarter Highway. It was hard keeping him at the speed limit. He kept saying we were being tailed. Got me thinking it too every time someone stayed behind us more than five minutes. He'd turn off the highway. Then on again. Sometimes he'd go in circles on neighborhood streets. Kind of thing that could attract cops. Worse still he kept yapping about stickup gangs and their brutal revenge. Told some gory payback stories he heard. Said they got snitches all over— which is probably how he got set up in the first place.

"So I asked him did he say I'd be coming along for the pickup. Had to yell it a couple times like he was going deaf. Finally he leveled. Said he talked me up big. Thought he was doing a favor. Might've even mentioned where I lived. The neighborhood. It took everything I had not to punch him out while he was driving. I made him drop me off behind the bar where we hooked up. Had my car parked there. He'd only stop a couple blocks across the street from it. And he took off soon as I closed the door. Never told him what I'd do next. Neither did—"

The rapid snap of branches has them sitting up, trying to locate the unfamiliar noises that seem to come from everywhere. Crows overhead call loudly to each other. Two black smudges race along the park canopy and the night sky. They dive at a larger, much bulkier figure soaring across the river, melting into the night and the eventual quiet.

"Must've been an owl after the chicks," Paul says, "They're night hunters."

"We should get going too."

Paul stands first and offers a hand up. Hal walks around testing his ankle. "Nice job, doc. Almost good as new."

They leave the park fast with Hal leading the way. Franklin Avenue's dead quiet. So's the hospital construction site they approach off Mill Street. Tractors and bulldozers stand near shallow ditches set behind a long, makeshift fence. "They remind me of dinosaurs," Paul says.

"Me too." Hal leads him to some trucks parked near a large green trailer that faces the street. Behind it, waiting in shadow, is his dark blue Mercury.

"You're lucky it didn't rain tonight," Paul says. "You could've got stuck in the mud."

"Like I never thought of that." Hal shows the beginnings of relief once they're inside the car. His face softens. His body seems to sink into the worn, upholstered seat. He shakes his head at some private thought and kisses the steering wheel. "For good luck." He starts the engine and deftly works his way around the trailer and onto Mill Street. He makes a right on Franklin and idles.

"I need to leave you here."

"Where you going?"

Hal shrugs. "Anyplace far away from Newark."

"What about graduation?"

"What about it?"

"Nothing, I guess."

"I'll figure the school thing out later, along with the rest."

"The rest of what?"

"Where to settle once I'm on the road. Think I might head west. Head straight to California right to the Pacific. Ain't that where people go to make a new start? I got the scratch now, thanks to you."

"People can start over in a lot of places. They don't have to travel far."

"There's plenty choice weed in L.A, it being so close to the border. Wouldn't take long to make the right contacts."

"That doesn't sound like a new start."

"It won't be the same," Hal says. "I'll work it much smarter this time, lower my risk close to zilch."

"You can say that after what happened last night?"

"There's much safer ways to make money in this business."

"Give me a for instance," Paul says. "Since you're no letter writer."

"For one thing, I could be a trucker for an importer. I hear they make big green for a single haul up here and back. A sawbuck for every ten pounds they carry. I hear each truck holds more than a ton. We're talking over 20

297

grand! A couple hauls'd set me up good for a year. I ain't greedy. And I'm a good driver. Now that's what I call a solid hedge."

"How'll you meet these importers and get them to trust you with so much?"

"I'll figure it out, don't you worry."

"So it's all okay then." Paul lifts his backpack off the floor and reaches for the door.

Hal grabs him by his nape and gathers him in an awkward embrace. One that isn't shared. "Maybe I'll surprise you and write when I'm settled out there. You can come for a visit. We'll have a good time together. You might even want to stay."

"That sounds great," Paul says. "I'm looking forward to it already."

ACKNOWLEDGMENTS

My thanks to Louis Flint Ceci for carefully shepherding this book to publication. Also my appreciation to the Gelman Library of The George Washington University for giving me full access to its resources.

ABOUT THE AUTHOR

Lou Dellaguzzo's work has appeared in *Hot Metal Bridge*, *ImageOutWrite*, *Hinchas De Poesia*, *Jonathan*, *Glitterwolf*, *Chroma*, *HGMLQ*, *Blithe House Quarterly*, and *Velvet Mafia*. He has also been published in *Best Gay Stories* 2014, 2016, and 2017; and in two editions of *Best Gay Love Stories* and *Best Gay Romance*. In 2011, his chapbook, *The Hex Artist*, won first place in the Treehouse Press (London) Fiction Contest. His collection of short stories, *The Island of No Secrets and Other Stories*, came out in 2019. He lives in Washington, DC, with his partner, and is currently working on an ensemble novel set in 1960s New York City.

CPSIA information can be obtained
at www.ICGtesting.com
Printed in the USA
BVHW032136250320
576034BV00001B/11